DIGGING FOR GOLD:

Papers on Archaeology for Profit

© 1976 Regents of The University of Michigan
The Museum of Anthropology
All rights reserved

Printed in the
United States of America

TABLE OF CONTENTS

Introduction: Archaeology and the Profits of Research
        William K. Macdonald...............vii

Contract Archaeology and the University
        Thomas J. Riley................... 1

Contract Cultural Resource Management: The Perspective
 of a State Archaeologist
        James E. Fitting...................18

Problems in the Organization and Growth of Corporate
 Archaeology
        William K. Macdonald
        Alex H. Townsend...................35

The Acquisition of Archaeological Contracts
        Alex H. Townsend...................52

Contract Archaeology from the Outside
        Steven A. LeBlanc..................72

ACKNOWLEDGMENTS

The initial impetus for this volume came from Dr. Richard Ford, Director of the Museum of Anthropology, University of Michigan. In the course of its preparation I have received much advice, assistance, and cooperation. I am especially grateful to Dr. Karl Hutterer, University of Michigan, and Dr. Alex H. Townsend, National Heritage Corporation for their encouragement. Typing and duplication of manuscripts was provided by John Milner, AIA, National Heritage Corporation; Patricia Ripley suffered through the multiple typings of nastily marked drafts. My effort and interest in the ethical and practical developments of the discipline are a result of my contact with H.D. Tuggle and R.J. Pearson. It is appropriate that this volume be dedicated, without the consent or knowledge of the authors herein, to Giovanni Belzoni, the first of the notorious contract archaeologists.

INTRODUCTION: ARCHAEOLOGY AND THE PROFITS OF RESEARCH

William K. Macdonald
University of Michigan

The express purpose of this collection of papers is, quite frankly, to raise some hackles among archaeologists. The discipline is undergoing a difficult time and, in accordance with Murphy's Law (i.e., *ceteris paribus* "things will get worse"), only the most optimistic predictions suggest that conditions will remain the same.

The recent past has seen a significant and traumatic shift in the theoretical perspective of many archaeologists in the United States. This has necessitated a reappraisal of organizational structures as well as methodological procedures. At the same time, long overdue legislative developments concerning conservation, preservation, and disposition of cultural resources, and restructuring of priorities by traditional granting institutions have totally and irrevocably changed the relationship of the discipline to the outside world. Relevance has assumed practical as well as theoretical import. Finally, the employment situation in archaeology has steadily deteriorated in the past few years. As recently as five years ago the job prospects of a bright young doctoral student were quite good; a similar situation is unlikely to recur in the future.

These three problem areas, changing perspectives, legislative developments, and rising unemployment, have often led to bitter debates concerning archaeology for hire. The papers below are aimed at defining the major areas of concern in what has come to be called contract archaeology. No single program for resolution of the discipline's ills is suggested here; the problems are too new. The goal of this collection is to generate discussion by posing questions rather than by answering them.

There are undoubtedly as many "solutions" to these problems as there are people who have considered them, archaeologists and others. And if this is even minimally true, then the papers here should provoke discussion. If such discussion leads to any progress within the discipline in dealing with its problems, then these papers will have served their purpose. Hopefully, a year or two will prove this volume out of date.

The volume began with a paper (Macdonald and Townsend, this volume) presented at a symposium of the Society of Historical Archaeology in January, 1976 on problems in archaeology as a profession. The problems we discussed in that paper were, in my view, crucial to the future of the discipline. Yet, when I began to solicit participation for this volume, I was surprised to find a great deal of apathy and/or timidity among archaeologists. The former attitude was most common among those academic archaeologists who seemingly wouldn't soil their hands with contract work; the latter attitude seemed widespread among archaeologists who had contractual or other positions to protect. Surely there are some whom I did not contact who would have been willing to contribute. There are also some whom I contacted who were quite simply overcommitted and who could not spare the time. It is interesting to note that almost

70 percent of the total membership polled on the question of a professional registry by the Society for American Archaeology didn't bother to respond. Presumably, there is a strong positive correlation between nonrespondants and employed archaeologists. Needless to say, the writers of the papers below lack both timidity and apathy.

In addition to concern and a willingness to stick out one's neck, a further consideration which prompted me to contact the authors presented here was a desire to solicit a diversity of opinion and experience. Regional problems in contract work have given rise to a variety of approaches and perspectives. Riley and LeBlanc are academics; Townsend is a corporate archaeologist for National Heritage Corporation; Fitting has been an academic and a state archaeologist, and is at present a corporate archaeologist with a large engineering firm, Commonwealth Associates, Inc. Geographically, Riley works largely in the Midwest, LeBlanc in the Southwest, Townsend in the Southeast and East, and Fitting in the Midwest and East. Temporally, Riley and LeBlanc are prehistorians; Townsend is an historical archaeologist; and Fitting has worked in both areas. My own experience has been as a contract and corporate archaeologist working with historic sites primarily in regions east of the Mississippi. As a result of these differences, this volume should be viewed not as a polemic, but rather as a set of polemics written by a disparate group of archaeologists who are concerned by recent developments in the field and thus have experiential axes to grind.

Despite the fact that the contributors are such a disparate group, and that they didn't see or discuss each other's papers prior to publication, there seems to be a number of points common to all of the papers. While there is certainly divergence of opinion among the writers (for example, I disagree with some points in all of the papers but my own), it may be appropriate at the outset to emphasize these recurrent themes.

Lack of Communication

No one knows the extent to which archaeology for profit is practiced in this country. Yet the progress of the discipline is highly dependent upon the wide and rapid dissemination of information. While there is some sort of grapevine which spreads rumors of who is doing or, more frequently, who has done what, where and when, the process is hit or miss at best. The incredible amount and pace of contracted work is such that it is virtually impossible to keep track of it, even for relatively circumscribed areas. If archaeologists don't know of their coworkers in a given area, how can the results of research be disseminated? How can individual research projects be integrated and synthesized? And how is the discipline to progress?

Competitive Bidding and Pricing of Research

Not only do contracted workers rarely know their colleagues, but little is generally known about how contracts are awarded. It is doubtful whether many archaeologists in the academic community have ever heard of National Heritage or Commonwealth Associates. It is also doubtful that competitive bidding which awards a specific contract to the lowest submitted budget, does much to raise the standard of research for hire. How bidders are chosen in noncompetitive situations is frequently unclear and often the result of capricious and shifting criteria. Townsend's firm, for example, was once underbid by more than $150,000 on a project but has also been awarded contracts as the highest bidder.

The general feeling is that competitive bidding can only result in a lowering of the quality of research. Money is tangible time; the less time spent on a project the lower the quality of the results, i.e., the less useful to the discipline as a whole. Unfortunately the reverse is not true. Yet, in archaeology, unlike a number of other disciplines, the point of diminishing returns for analysis of recovered data costs far in excess of what any contracting agency can or will pay. The obvious result is a sharp decrease in analytical time and a concomitant minimizing of the research potential of a given site or series of sites.

Ethics

In archaeology, ethics has most often been directed to aspects of conduct among archaeologists, and has rarely, if ever been applied to the relationship with the nonarchaeological community. Only recently, with the rise of minority rights groups, have archaeologists begun to realize that they have obligations to groups other than themselves. But the demands of the outside and, to the archaeologist, very unreal world require consistent and high ethical standards. The real world of archaeology in this century, at least, is the sheltered halls of the university or museum, but this is rapidly changing and will continue to change as money becomes increasingly available from nontraditional sources. Archaeologists must come to grips with the problems inherent in dealing with the world outside. Yet few have asked what our obligation to the nonarchaeological community is specifically to be. How can archaeologists collect, analyze, and present data as anthropologists and scientists with a just regard for themselves not only to those for whom those data represent cultural properties, but also to those who pay for the research and, most importantly perhaps, to the public at large?

Splitting the Discipline

Most of the authors here seem concerned that a split in the discipline between theoretical academics and applied contractors and data collectors is a maladaptive dichotomizing which will not resolve any problems and will probably cause additional ones. It is felt that such a split will discourage innovation, comparison, and synthesis in the nonacademic sphere. Whether one agrees with this presumed result or not, we should be aware that this division is very real, albeit somewhat hazy at present. If such a split becomes final, as it has in many other disciplines, what are the implications for the development of archaeology as a whole? The impression that is given here is that academics do archaeology well in academia, but that archaeology done outside of academia is done poorly. But how can we estimate performance when we lack channels of communication which would allow adequate peer evaluation? It is obvious and crucial that archaeologists: 1) ask themselves hard questions about contract work and its implications for the discipline, 2) devise criteria, exclusive of organizational and structural ones, by which contracted work may be judged, and 3) take a close look at disciplines (such as chemistry, geology and engineering) which have split, survived and continued to advance. We must develop models to provide for the advancement of the discipline.

While these points may be common in the papers below, they are not unanimous. The only unity provided in this volume is to be found in the strong opinion of the authors that change must come about, and quickly, in order for archaeology to continue to progress as a viable and worthwhile discipline. Hopefully, this volume is a first step in the initiation of such change.

CONTRACT ARCHAEOLOGY AND THE UNIVERSITY

Thomas J. Riley
University of Illinois
Urbana, Illinois

At the 1975 S.A.A. meetings in Dallas, Texas, a public discussion took place on the subject of a National Registry of Professional Archaeologists. At one point in the heated debate a S.A.A. member stood to make a distinction between professional and university archaeologists. His thesis was that only a researcher engaged in year-round field archaeology should be considered a professional. This eliminates from the category the faculty member who spends only part of his time in the field and the rest of it in training students and writing heady theoretical articles. I take this to mean that the university archaeologist has not taken an active part in contract archaeology, for it is certainly true that faculty members have actively engaged in research in all parts of the world under the auspices of granting organizations such as NSF, Ford, and Rockefeller Foundations.

I do not consider the distinction between the professional and university archaeologist a valid one. The archaeologist working in a university context certainly faces a number of unique problems when confronted with the current state of contract archaeology. The university operates under a set of constraints, many having nothing to do with the practice of field archaeology, which are different from those of corporations or museums. The archaeologist faculty member must live within these constraints.

Most anthropology departments today focus on teaching the requisite skills of the discipline's various parts, on faculty research and publications, and on the difficult job of maintaining themselves against the pressure to cut existing human and physical resources. The university archaeologist is either an integral part of this scene or else quickly finds a job in a museum or, perhaps nowadays, in a corporation. As a result university archaeologists have often found it difficult to deal with funding sources outside the traditional academic research sphere.

Changing patterns of funding for archaeological research, however, are leading university archaeologists into contract relationships with government agencies. However, several obstacles confront the university archaeologist who wishes to enter the complex web of federal and state archaeological contract relations. Three of the most obvious involve: a) development of adequate research designs for contract research; b) scheduling of contract work; and c) implementation of research and analysis within the structure of the university.

Contract Research Design

The design of research goals and methods is the first important step in carrying out any worthwhile and successful archaeological research program. In this area, the academic archaeologist most often has a distinct advantage over colleagues in museum and corporate situations. The academic has traditionally been in the enviable position of being able to concentrate on particular problems of individual interest rather than those defined by agents of the outside world.

Lipe (1974) has pointed out that academics have only the archaeological problem defining their research. Problems of their own choosing motivate the research design, the tactics for implementation of that design, and the presentation of the final product. This internal motivation is one of the reasons a number of archaeologists enter and remain in the groves of academe rather than face the harsh realities of the museum, civil service, or corporate contexts where they would be constrained by influences over which they have little control. The university archaeologist, for example, has freedom of choice in research area and goals seldom reached in museums or corporations.

The museum or corporate archaeologist must often implement archaeological survey in areas that are relatively unknown, limited by road alignments or purchase boundaries, and hampered as well by the fact that finished descriptive work is expected in sixty days or so with little time to conduct sufficient analysis of the materials recovered and processed. Some contractors expect a detailed analytical report in a short period of time yet provide inadequate funds for analysis.

In contrast, the academic archaeologist's monies are directly related to a particular problem which in turn is directly related to the positive evaluation of a research design by colleagues at NSF or a similar funding agency. The academic receives reinforcement on the worth of the design and his ability to carry the problem to its resolution by peer acceptance at different levels. The academic can run data through sets of test implications like laundry through a wringer, consolidating every bit of support for final formulations. This may take several years or a lifetime. If the continuing results of the research are considered worthwhile, the academic will be repeatedly funded to continue that direction of research.

A second characteristic of traditional academic problem-oriented research design is that the researcher is only committed to gathering and processing information which is relevant to a particular problem. Even though most of us have been taught that we should be gathering, processing, and describing archaeological materials so that they may be applicable to many research problems, the common fact of life is that the researcher working on "pure" research pays more attention to those facets of data relevant to a specific problem, sometimes with little regard for its descriptive worth to others with different interests in the field. The academic researcher working with noncontract funds can afford this luxury, although it might be argued that such a luxury is inimical to synthetic statements.

The contract researcher cannot be so specific in data processing techniques: contract archaeology is most often done under emergency salvage conditions. The contract researcher, even if unable to process much of the data that is recovered, must be cognizant of the potential of that data for other researchers. Sites excavated in such research are often lost forever under highways, dams, housing subdivisions or similar philistine enterprises. All this seems to make the academic archaeologist's position an enviable one indeed, but may promote the spurious dichotomy between academic archaeologist and those who would consider themselves "professionals."

There are certain psychological benefits available to those in academia pursuing so-called "pure" academic research in archaeology. The well established academic archaeologist does not want to give up professional autonomy in designing research or the satisfaction of producing a piece of work which has been blessed by his peers. He often considers contract archaeology to be beneath him, and thus reinforces the dichotomy between academic and professional researchers.

Scheduling of Research

A second major problem for the university archaeologist engaging in contract work is not psychological but tactical. Archaeological contracts, especially those involving emergency salvage, are often scheduled within the framework of a larger engineering problem designed to complete a public work in the fastest time possible over a predetermined number of years. Only a small part of the schedule of the entire project is given over to archaeological research. Research must be conducted not only before land alteration takes place, but also within the schedule of the contract as a whole. While initial Environmental Impact Statements may verbally guarantee that emergency salvage will be conducted before construction begins, little attention is paid to the time that archaeology takes. The required research is often impossible to carry out during the summer months alone.

Museum and corporate archaeological structures are geared to conduct research within the time schedules mandated by the contracting agency. They can gear up for a twenty-six week field season that will begin in early spring and end in late fall. (In the Southeast and in states like Hawaii, fieldwork is carried out all year round.)

In contrast, academic researchers are limited by schedules imposed by their institutions. They are usually under a nine month contract with a university, with three months free for conducting research or teaching during the summer. Even then, if state employees, they may be enjoined from conducting research for any more than two months during the summer. Thus, the difficulty in coordinating the university schedule with an external schedule prevents the faculty member from taking otherwise attractive contracts. The state university does not encourage its faculty to take a contract which would occupy the entire three months of faculty free time. On the contrary, the university may discourage participation in contract archaeology by permitting its faculty only two months of summer research time.

The university faculty member can sometimes get around scheduling problems by taking a leave of absence, but this is often not feasible, especially in temperate climates because the field season ends by mid-November at the latest. If a granting agency would provide salaries for laboratory work until the beginning of a new field season, the faculty researcher might be able to maintain himself. However, the contracting agency is often unable or unwilling to fund a principal investigator in this way. In many instances, then, it is impossible to obtain research leave to conduct and complete a contract.

An additional aspect of the scheduling problem is presented by the summer research responsibilities of the university faculty member. Most departments sponsor a field school to which the academic archaeologist is committed for the summer sessions of the academic year. In some instances the field school may be tied into contract research, but in many situations the conduct of contract research is hostile to a learning environment. No innate antithesis exists between a field school research problem and a contract situation, but there is the potential of *using* students rather than teaching them. And teaching, in addition to the solution of a research problem in the archaeological remains under study, is certainly a primary goal of the faculty member conducting a field school of archaeology.

The most successful field schools in archaeology are those which integrate a long-term research design with the teaching of methods and techniques of field archaeology. A student cannot benefit from the instrumentation and mechanics of archaeological research unless he learns the end for which those mechanics are being used. The contract situation, in which time is as valuable as gold, sometimes reduces the student to slave status, and not even a wage slave at that. In such situations students learn their digging methods by rote, and may not fit them into the context of the expected results of the research because such expectations may never be introduced to them.

Implementation of Research and Analysis

A third obstacle to the conduct of contract archaeology within the university situation, and the last one that I will talk about here, is the lack of means to implement research and analysis. Implementing research is a problem endemic to the university situation because scheduling of students' time is much the same as that of the faculty member. Research assistantships and associateships generated by contracts could potentially benefit a graduate student in search of a research problem or area for the Master's degree or, in some cases, for the Ph.D.

The problem is that graduate student research interests and the specifics of contract archaeological situations seldom match. The students, their advisors, and the departments must make a choice between the contract situation and the situation that students consider ideal for exploring the problem that they have isolated for advanced degree research. The graduate student's situation is much the same as the faculty archaeologist's, except that the student has added pressure from the faculty advisor in deciding whether or not to follow up on a potential contract.

In addition, it is often difficult to raise an adequate work force for pursuing a large and lengthy but temporally limited contract in a university situation. Again, this is because students follow the same schedule as their professors, at least theoretically, and are usually unavailable in sufficient numbers for research conducted during the early spring and late fall.

These are mechanical obstacles but important ones. A much more critical problem is presented by the negotiation process that contracts often involve. The outcomes of contract negotiation can sometimes lead to problems in implementing analysis that the archaeologist considers necessary for the successful completion of a research program. Contracting agencies have a tendency to see the archaeological process as the recording

and physical removing of archaeological sites from the path of proposed
land alteration. They often fail to recognize the need for intensive
analysis of the remains recovered from the archaeological site. The
principal investigator must perforce justify to contracting agencies
the necessity for such analysis. The negotiation process can sometimes
be quite difficult, and the investigator may lose some of his proposed
research because the contracting agency views it as ephemeral in relation
to its main objective of getting the material out of the ground and
curated as fast, i.e., as cheaply, as possible.

Detailed analysis of those data specifically related to the
researcher's problems are the first items trimmed from the contract.
Without them, the hope of developing nomothetic statements from the
occupations under study is trimmed as well. All archaeologists find
this situation frustrating, but I think that it is most frustrating for
the museum and faculty archaeologists who are trying to integrate contract
archaeology with their investigation of a particular problem. The
corporate archaeologist can, I think, live within the limits imposed
by the contractor, because the corporation often has a more realistic
view of the needs of the agency and tailors its proposals to them. I
do know of some corporate archaeologists who have abandoned the corporate
sphere because of a feeling of frustration with the limited goals to
be achieved there.

I think that it is fair to say that these three obstacles cause
some academic archaeologists to shun the contract scene in American
archaeology if they possibly can, and they contribute to the validation

of the distinction between professional and academic archaeologists that has been made by some researchers.

Restructuring Academic Environments

I am not arguing that academics do not play a significant part in contract research. In fact, they play a large and important part in contract archaeology in many states. If they had their "druthers," though, I think it is fair to say many academics would leave the contract sphere to museum and corporate archaeologists and explore the problems that interest them. It is the harsh reality of funding that keeps the academic archaeologist in the contract sphere, and that reality has to be met by a restructuring of both the university and the contract environments to make the obvious implementation of research goals possible.

I would argue that the university archaeologist has an advantage over the corporate or the museum archaeologist, especially in certain locally defined situations. Some universities, the University of Missouri is an instance, have a Division of Archaeological Research or Laboratory of Anthropology that is the research arm of the Department of Anthropology. The research arm gets around the mechanical problems of staffing and scheduling of research by employing a small full-time field and analytical staff which can be supplemented by graduate students as their scheduling permits.

The academic archaeologist associated with the research arm of the department is in an ideal position to make the best use of research contracts within the scope of his research interests. Ideally, the contract research undertaken by the research arm of the department can provide supplemental information to test those hypotheses generated, and at least partially confirmed, by other, non-contract research.

This integration of research objectives, with contract archaeology supplementing and supporting research conducted in a non-contract millieu is, I think, best illustrated by the efforts of Stuart Struever, originator of the Foundation for Illinois Archaeology. His research in the Illinois River valley is focused on describing and explaining changing human adaptations within the valley (Struever 1968a, b). To this end, he has made use of a mixed bag of funding sources, ranging from private contributions to research contracts from state and federal agencies. The success of his program is largely due to the incorporation of contract archaeological research into a framework developed and maintained through non-contract funds. The Foundation for Illinois Archaeology has the flexibility necessary to make economical use of the contract situation. It is also in the position of being able to enhance the conclusions of its contract reports by the inclusion of information relevant to, but not generated by, the piece of contract research being presented.

The Foundation of Illinois Archaeology and the University of Missouri Division of Archaeological Research are only two specific examples of the restructuring of academic environments necessary to develop viable interfaces with the contract archaeology scene in America today. There are others, such as the Arkansas Archaeological Survey, that have adapted differently to the current environment. The important point to be made from these examples is that the research units have succeeded by restructing the relationships between the universities that house them and the environment out of which most archaeology in this country will soon be funded--the government contract agency.

Ideally, the research arm of a university should:

1. Be flexible in its ability to conduct research within the schedules of contractors;

2. Provide an adequate set of facilities for analysis and curation of recovered data;

3. Have a research interest (other than contract) in the area for which it accepts contracts so that both contract and non-contract research results can be integrated; and,

4. Have an infrastructure that is maintained primarily by funding outside the contract sphere.

All four of these considerations are important. The fourth, however difficult to achieve, seems to me most important in order to keep a university from becoming involved with more contracts than it can adequately handle or which are external to its research goals.

In order to make the university a suitable place for the conduct of contract research, contracting agencies must be restructured to some extent to permit a contract researcher to conduct the necessary analysis for fruitful conclusion of a particular piece of research. Funding the analysis of archaeological remains recovered from the excavated site must become a priority item in contract budgets.

If these two shifts can be made--first, the restructuring of the university environment so as to permit the academic archaeologist to work efficiently in a contract environment, and second, the shifting of contractor's priorities so as to permit the researcher to adequately analyze as well as process and curate materials recovered from the field--then the conduct of contract archaeology by the academic archaeologist becomes more profitable from the researcher's point of view. If these conditions are met, the contractor can get more information structured in a more coherent way from university archaeologists than from the corporate researcher.

The Benefits of Academic Archaeology

Given the shifts mentioned above, there are some definite benefits to conducting contract research under the aegis of the university. The first, and perhaps most important condition favoring the academic archaeologist in the conduct of contract research is a commitment to a problem and a research area. While the corporate archaeologist follows contracts for the maintenance of his section within the corporation, the academic archaeologist is relatively sedentary, following out the problems presented in a defined research area. Presumably the academic will conduct contract research only within a limited area of expertise. Thus, academic archaeologists are in a position to bring prior research results to bear on the problems presented by the contract research. They are also capable of incorporating the contract research into future exploration of problems in the prehistory or history of the contract sample area affected. The results should ideally result in a better understanding of the past in the contract area than would be possible from a corporate archaeologist, and in retrieval of data that will be efficiently used rather than raw information processed and stored for future use.

A second argument for conducting contract archaeology in an academic setting is implied in the broad resource base that the university represents. The research arm associated with the university has areas of expertise represented that are not available in the corporate setting, and are seldom possible in museums. Physical analytic techniques, faunal and floral analyses, soils and materials characterization, and other analyses can usually be conducted within the university without costly subcontracting. In fact, the contracting agency is tying into a network of resources within the university which is difficult to match in other environments without the expenditure of huge amounts of money.

The final reason to be cited here for conducting contract archaeology through the academy is the potential for the exercise of objective ethical judgments in the conduct of particular research. In a very real sense, the corporation is in a position subservient to the demands of the contractor. This is often true of the museum as well, especially where museums depend on contract research for the maintenance of their ongoing research programs. While the university in general is definitely dependent on grants for the maintenance of its programs, the particular faculty member is less subject to external constraints on his judgment about the feasibility of a particular grant or contract. The faculty archaeologist is in a position to have proposed research criticized and evaluated by departmental and university peers before it is approved. The faculty member is also in the position of being able to oppose any particular contract offer made from an outside agency, rather than accepting it as offered, and is at least theoretically protected in opposing a particular piece of research by the guidelines of academic freedom. This is a stance the corporate archaeologist cannot claim, and one sometimes difficult in a museum situation as well.

The position that any particular academic researcher takes in regard to the adequacy or justification of any contract is personal, of course, and will vary with the individual. I would argue, though, that the protection of the right to make ethical judgments about the acceptance or rejection of a piece of research as proposed is a strong, if not absolute, argument in favor of the conduct of archaeological research from the university setting.

Conclusions

I conclude only by saying that there are at present serious obstacles to the conduct of contract archaeology research within a university context. Some of these obstacles are mechanical, but the major obstacle is the unwillingness of university archaeologists to give up the autonomy of research they have enjoyed until the present time. It is essentially a psychological obstacle, and will only be overcome if: 1) there is a shift in the faculty member's relationship with the rest of the academic sphere so that the academic can comfortably pursue contract research, and 2) there is a shift in the attitudes of contracting agencies toward permitting the researcher to at least minimally follow up and solve anthropological problems of interest.

These shifts in structural relationships will not come easily, but where they do take place, the university can provide contractors with more information, more coherently organized, than the corporation and, in some instances, the museum can. At the same time, the university archaeologist is in a better position to defend, reject, and evaluate contracting programs than are colleagues in the museum or corporate spheres.

The dichotomy between the professional and the academic in archaeology is at present a spurious one. It could, however, become a real division. Faculty archaeologists who refuse to attempt to integrate their problems with the contract scene in North America are contributing to its validation. We are warned that the majority of archaeological funding in the future will be from contract sources. It is our responsibility to see that basic research into problems of human behavior and its correlates are continued in the context of this change in funding emphases.

REFERENCES

Lipe, William D.

    1974   A conservation model for American archaeology. In Kiva 39:213-45.

Struever, Stuart

    1968a Woodland subsistence-settlement systems in the lower Illinois Valley. In New Perspectives in Archaeology, Sally R. and Lewis R. Binford, eds. Aldine: Chicago, pp. 285-312.

    1968b Problems, methods and organization: a disparity in the growth of archaeology. In Anthropological archaeology in the Americas, Betty J. Meggers, ed. Anthropological Society of Washington, pp. 131-51.

CONTRACT CULTURAL RESOURCE MANAGEMENT:
THE PERSPECTIVE OF A STATE ARCHAEOLOGIST

James E. Fitting
Commonwealth Associates, Inc.
Jackson, Michigan

When invited to prepare a statement on how a state archaeologist views the changing nature, and even name, of the current archaeological "crisis" associated with cultural resource management, my first reaction was, "but I am not a state archaeologist anymore!" Under my breath I muttered the usual prayers of thanks and relief that I have come to associate with this statement and awaited the withdrawal of the request. It was not forthcoming: instead, I was told that a number of state archaeologists had been asked to write this chapter and all had declined to do so.

Perhaps it would have been the better part of valor to act in the same manner but by doing so, a very important point of view might be lost. An ex-state archaeologist may also be in a better position to express the concerns of state archaeologists who, should they speak out, could suffer the wrath of both bureaucratic supervisors and academic colleagues. Therefore, the following pages are historical comments on a three-year term I served as state archaeologist, the problems encountered over this time period, and the lack of resolution I saw, and still see, to these problems. In every sense of the phrase, these are the "confessions of an ex-state archaeologist."

In 1972, I accepted the position of state archaeologist in a fairly populous and prosperous midwestern state. Although it was a personal economic disaster to do so, the position seemed to have a number of other advantages over teaching. For one thing, I had a deep and long-standing interest in the archaeology of that state. After ten years of teaching in major universities, I was also disillusioned with the university as a place where one might obtain an education. The goals of perpetuating the existing state of ignorance, protecting the balkanization of the academic community into tribal departments, and the perpetual rationalizing of self-serving positions under the guise of "educational integrity" were all too poorly disguised. A non-academic position, protected by civil service rather than the capriciousness of tenure and contracts seemed, in the long run, more secure, if less financially rewarding.

There were very few skill models available for state archaeologists at that time. Those that were available were primarily successful individuals. Bill Ritchie, in particular, was a state archaeologist to whom I turned for a skill model in the early days of this career. Through thick and thin, Ritchie had maintained an ongoing research program, managed to publish at least one major report almost every year, and had prepared an excellent synthesis of the archaeology of his state.

There were also some ongoing problems that were constant sources of irritation to me as a state archaeologist. They furnished the background against which the changing role was played. These problems were primarily fiscal and all were interrelated. There were a number of professional archaeologists in the state who wished the state to put money into archaeology, but believed that it should be done by increasing university and college programs rather than supporting the state program. During the early years in particular, I was often telephoned by a legislative aid or secretary of my acquaintence who would tell me that a delegation of professors had been in to lobby for the elimination of my job. Members of these delegations would later assure me that their efforts were not directed against me personally. While they never succeeded, their attempts made it difficult to argue for increased support for a state archaeological program. In fact, it confused the issue sufficiently to insure that the state archaeologist never did, and probably never will, receive a specific legislative appropriation in that state.

It seems to me that this was simply a reflection of a larger problem within archaeology. Archaeologists are one of the few groups that destroy a portion of the material which they study. This leads to a quest for more detail in recording contextual data as it is being destroyed which, in turn, must be weighed against the limited time and budgets that archaeologists must meet in carrying out this destruction. No archaeologist worth his salt is ever satisfied with his own work. How, then, can he be satisfied with the work of any other archaeologist? Most expressions of approbation directed by archaeologists to one another are really statements to the effect that a member of the profession had done a better job than we thought him capable of, or that he did things almost as well as we would have, had we been the ones doing it. This attitude permeates archaeological thinking and archaeologists understand it. Nonarchaeologists, particularly those in positions in which planning decisions are paramount, do not understand it. Their reaction is simply to wish for a pox to fall on the houses of all of the bickering pack.

It was against this background that my position on contract support for cultural resource management developed. In retrospect, I see this as a constant awakening to many of the difficulties of carrying out archaeological work in a changing universe. Not all state archaeologists have passed through the phases of development which I did, and I am certain that others have experienced problems which I did not face. However, the information exchange on occasions such as the meetings of state archaeologists held in conjunction with those of the Society for American Archaeology over the past few years, indicates to me that many of the problems are similar.

In the early 1970s, the effects of NEPA and Executive Order 11593 began to be felt in the archaeological community. During my first few months as state archaeologist, I was approached by a number of federal agencies and private firms for archaeological information. Since I viewed the position as basically a service position, I offered all the help that I could as a part of my job. There were some weeks during which I worked 120 hours, often driving several thousand miles in order to walk power lines and check construction sites as much as 400 miles apart.

Some of the groups seeking advice were most helpful and suggested that they might be able to make small financial contributions to cover travel expenses and hire part-time staff if this might lead to more rapid production of the information they desired. At the time, this seemed like a satisfactory solution and donations ranging from several hundred to several thousand dollars were added to the "gift fund" of the agency within which I was housed. These were used to add support staff for a variety of small projects.

I was quite used to grant research from my years within universities. Both public and private foundations expected institutional cost sharing for such programs and it seemed logical that if an outside source contributed to fieldwork, the agency should expect to pick up part of the tab for typing, telephone calls, staff benefits and other similar expenses. After all, we had been doing the work entirely at our own expense and any outside contribution was better than none.

In a traditional academic sense, we were well on our way to developing a "successful" program. That is, we were supporting more and more people on soft money, preparing more reports more rapidly, and accumulating valuable "research" collections. Notice the change from what I had been doing to what we were then doing; we were well on our way to developing the bright green research machine, the "Institute" that is the secret goal of most archaeologists.

The very "success" in the traditional sense that this applies to an archaeological program, led to a much closer evaluation of the program than I ever had to face before, and a number of internal forces were building within it. First, and foremost was the growing recognition of the real cost of doing archaeology. I did not see this at the time and objected strongly to it when it was pointed out to me. A state employee received fifteen days of paid vacation and fifteen days of sick leave each year, a totally subsidized retirement program and a near totally subsidized insurance program. While regular positions were limited by the budget, even part-time positions required staff benefits. Putting five people on part-time, or in full-time temporary positions, took enough out of the overall operating budget to eliminate one full-time position.

What is more, pressure began to be felt by typists, editors, duplication facilities and, above all, those responsible for providing space. Space was needed for desks, work tables and collection storage areas. Many of these problems could be solved on a temporary basis. State Museum storage areas were converted to laboratories and offices, and metal microfilm cabinets, abandoned with the conversion to a computerized driver license system, were ideal for collections. However, we had no staff for moving and storing collections since everyone was involved in report preparation or project administration. It became clear that even larger amounts of money would be necessary to keep the operation going. The project funds were the easiest part to come by.

It also turned out to be too easy to underestimate the cost of analysis and report preparation. This was done on study after study and, of course, the state picked up the tab for these cost overruns. This was usually paid for in the form of my salary, or of more hours of my time above that for which I was being paid. The part-time and temporary people vanished when the funds were gone. The real cost of doing archaeology was coming home.

Problems in four areas led to the eventual termination of this program. They developed independently but were actually related. The first had to do with fiscal crises in all areas of state government and the effects of a closer scrutiny of how monies were being spent. We could show work reports with almost a dozen full-time equivalents working on archaeological projects when we were budgeted for only two positions! Where was the money coming from and how did we do this? As it turned out, we were not the only agency which had such "slush funds" as they were termed by the auditors. I suppose we called more attention to them by proposing several contracts in excess of $20,000 with obligations to be paid as contributions to the gift fund. This was too obvious, and the auditors pointed out that we could not have state agencies doing business on their own without legislative control. It was determined that we still could accept gifts, but that such gifts would go directly into the state general fund, like taxes, and would be reallocated to agencies as a part of the state budget. If we accepted such assignments, we would not receive the money and would be required to carry out the work with appropriate funds. I came close to doing a $25,000 contract by myself as a result of this ruling. Never before, or since, have I been so delighted at having a project awarded to someone else.

We also had increasing difficulties with the personnel office. There had always been the problem of reconciling the start of the fiscal year on July 1 with the delay of the budget approval until September of that year. Usually, the previous years' budget would be carried over for regular civil service positions but not for soft money positions. Therefore, my summer field crews were terminated on July 1 each year!

In order to maintain a field program, I started prehiring them in March, started them working in June and kept them in the field until August while passing out pay checks two months late. I almost ended up in jail over that tactic, although I had discussed it with my superiors and the personnel office before I started doing it. It seems that they were being audited as well, and the legal complications of signing payroll forms for people who were not working in the spring, and having people working who were not covered by liability insurance in the fall, were considerations which we had neglected.

We made a half-hearted attempt to carry on with personal service contracts after this time. It took approximately three months to approve a small contract, so small jobs were out of the question. It took a full-time administrator to monitor a large personal service contract and prepare the audit forms on progress payments. We faced the dual problems of contractors who defaulted on preparing reports, after receiving 90 percent or more of their progress payments, and of contractors threatening to sue us when their progress payments were held up for auditing. It just did not work

Another factor which led to the elimination of hiring part-time and temporary people was the rising unemployment in 1974 and an increased awareness of the cost of unemployment insurance. We found that we were liable for unemployment insurance payments for a period equal to that which an employee had worked. The size of these payments was determined by factors beyond our control and we might be responsible for a larger weekly unemployment benefit than we had paid an employee when he or she was working. This never happened on one of my programs but it did on other programs. One colleague received a grant for $70,000, which required special legislative approval to keep it from going into the state general fund. He immediately had <u>half</u> of it placed in a special holding account to cover eventual unemployment claims. Had I done any further contract work through the state, this would have been the procedure followed with my projects as well.

If this fiscal problem were not enough, legal problems became a second area of major concern. By 1973, there were commercial firms engaged in cultural resources management. Some very real questions arose about whether government employees supported by tax dollars should work in competition with the private sector. It was viewed as being similar to the state operating its own oil wells and refineries and selling cut rate gas in competition with existing companies. It would amount to socializing archaeology within a free enterprise system. Interestingly enough, the question was first raised by several archaeologists with the university system who seemed to forget that they were also working at tax supported institutions although, in effect, they were allowed to operate small businesses within them.

An even more evident legal problem arose in the area of review. As federal legislation and regulations became more effective, the state archaeologist was called upon to review more reports, application permits and environmental impact statements. There is an inherent contradiction in being asked to review your own reports. It is like grading your own papers; of course you put down all of the correct answers! There is even more of a contradiction if you are competing with other groups for the dollars to prepare the reports which you will review. Many of our clients in those years, as I look back at it, came to us not because of our expertise or price, but because we would be almost certain to favorably review our own work. This was the final and most convincing argument against the involvement of state archaeologists in contract work of any sort. It inevitably leads to the weakening of the integrity of the entire review system. Even the most honorable of individuals will not be above the suspicion of favoring his own reports above those of others.

A third problem also resulted from additional review responsibilities. The review function became a larger and larger part of the job until it far outweighed any other function of the state archaeologist. First came the major federal Environmental Impact Statements (EIS), then the state Environmental Impact Statements. These were followed by integration into the A-95 review process and then by reviews required for Corps of Engineers permits and even state permits.

EIS review was fairly easy. These came in at the rate of approximately fifty a year while I was state archaeologist. One could be read, the files and literature checked, and an appropriate response prepared in approximately eight hours of working time for a good sized EIS. Corps permits came in at the rate of approximately twenty per week; other permit applications were just beginning to come in when I left the position. These could be reviewed at a rate of three or more an hour.

The most difficult task was A-95 review. There were some weeks when as many as 450 projects would be listed on the review sheets. In a forty hour week, this allows a little over five minutes of review time per project which was not even enough time to check the site files on all projects. Taken together and added to other tasks that a state archaeologist must perform (site file development, National Register nomination, preparation of popular and technical literature, talks to school groups and routine housekeeping tasks), there were just not enough hours in the week to do all of the review associated with the position, let along engage in either pure or contract research.

So the bright green research machine rusted and in its place was a desk piled high with papers. I do not see how it could or should have happened any other way. It is this very important review function that will make or break the entire process of wisely managing and developing the cultural resource base of the country. Someone has to stay home and mind the shop while others go out with their shovels.

There is a side effect of staying home to mind the store. To some extent, you are removed from the bickering archaeologist syndrome. You start evaluating archaeological studies not by what you would do, since you know you cannot do anything, but by 1) what other archaeologists are doing, 2) the legal requirements of the studies, and 3) what the client paying for the report and the reviewing agencies are after. My first reaction was to be thankful when there was any type of cultural resource evaulation in an environmental study. When I was last reviewing such documents in 1975, probably as much as 70 percent made no mention of cultural resources and another 15 percent contained such banalities as, "if any cultural resources are encountered during construction, a professional archaeologist will be consulted." These statements were the areas of greatest concern to me as a state archaeologist, but I found that many academic archaeologists were more concerned with the "adequacy" of the remaining 15 percent of the reports than with the majority which expressed no concern. A literature search and projection of sensitive zones is far better than nothing in such reports and this was achieved or added for many studies only after weeks of delay and acrimony on the part of state and federal agencies, and private firms who claimed, quite legitimately, that they had no funds for such work.

Once I was in the position where it was no longer possible to carry out primary field evaulations of sites I ran into the fourth problem area: work load flow with outside contractors. After spending close to a year negotiating for an archaeological survey with one federal agency, I found that no archaeologist within the state was interested in doing the survey. They were all too busy with their problems or with other contracts. In short, they were interested in contract work to the extent that it supported projects in which they had a personal interest rather than state-wide problems of cultural resource management.

In several instances, blatant ethical problems were encountered that could be evaulated without written rules. In the situation described above, one archaeologist agreed to carry out the survey if paid at the rate of $300 per day for the work, since it would take time away from a more interesting research project. In another instance, an archaeologist recommended $10,000 to $20,000 for a mitigation in his survey report, but expressed no interest in actually doing the mitigation. After five months of negotiation involving federal and state agencies and the outside advice of five professional archaeologists, a budget of $70,000 was developed for a mitigation with a less than five percent sample of the sites. This was weighed against the cost of relocating the facility which could be done for $7,000. A memorandum of agreement was signed relocating the facility to avoid the site. Several weeks later, the original survey archaeologist, who had declined to participate in developing the mitigation cost plans, contacted the federal agency directly and offered to carry out the mitigation utilizing a summer field school, for less than the cost of relocating the facility. Representatives from the federal agency reported this to me and expressed their confusion over the situation. This particular agency has since avoided dealing with any archaeologists because, as one representative worded it, "they do not appear to have any professional standards."

While serving as state archaeologist I also had the experience of serving as contract officer for a number of projects carried on throughout the state. If the experiences which I had are similar to those experienced by federal agencies and private firms, I can see why they have developed an "archaeophobia." In no instance, no matter what size the project, was a report completed by the deadline specified in the contract. The time delay caused by this report delinquincy cost the state more, in terms of project delays, than the cost of the original reports.

In only one instance was a report prepared in a format which could be circulated. All other reports were disorganized, poorly written (if written at all) and poorly illustrated. The state had to expend thousands of dollars editing, rewriting, retyping, and preparing illustrations for such reports. In one instance, we received a one line statement that the collections from an excavated site were not significant enough to require a report on the work that had been carried out there. This happened to be test excavation adjacent to one of the oldest standing buildings in the state.

Unfortunately, most of these contractors were paid if they turned in any type of report since the state archaeologist's office was under the pressure of the accounting office to close out these jobs within one or two years after the date of completion of the contract. I understand that since I left the position, one contractor was actually refused payment after he turned in an unintelligible report dealing with something other than he had been contracted to perform. I hope that we can see more of this in the future.

The major problem with contract archaeology is the archaeologist. Most contract studies ask for very specific information that is to be used in planning. The contracting agency is often provided with a document which might be of interest to another archaeologist but is of little use in the implementation of planning programs. It often purports to be a cultural resource study even though only prehistoric sites are considered. It is usually a costly document in terms of its use to a planner. And it is usually delivered late, often in a form unsuitable for public distribution.

Where does the state archaeologist stand in this matter? He is, of course, in the middle. The state archaeologist must never fall behind in EIS review, permit applications, or A-95 lists. The state archaeologist has the primary responsibility for operating the early warning system on potentially destructive situations. If sites are lost, it is usually the state archaeologist who is blamed for it. The state archaeologist must work with private and public planners in incorporating archaeological, historical, and architectural information into larger programs. The state archaeologist must serve as an interpreter of archaeological jargon to the nonarchaeological community.

Ideally, the state archaeologist should be a part of the group that considers the cost/benefit ratios of projects and there are times when cultural resources must take a secondary position to other pressing demands within the larger social context. In such instances, the state archaeologist will be the recipient of the wrath of the archaeological community for "allowing" a two-chip site to be destroyed. This is based on actual experience. I once received a very irate letter from an academic archaeologist for approving the construction of a four inch pipeline through a 20 acre field where two flint chips had been found.

The state archaeologist sits on a fence, open to the brickbats that any engineer, planner or archaeologist wishes to throw. It is a thankless position with major losses and no victories, at least no victories associated with traditional archaeological rewards. In contrast to positions within the federal government, most state archaeologists are underpaid and certainly overworked. With few exceptions, the salary range for a 12-month, forty hour plus work week, is within that of a starting assistant professor. It takes a strong constitution and limitless dedication to hold such a position in the face of the widespread irrationality of the archaeological community which the state archaeologist is supposed to represent and which usually will not support him in a crisis.

Those states which have a functioning, and still sane, state archaeologist are lucky. This is the person who will organize and evaluate contract work in terms of specific cultural resource management goals. It is as useless for the state archaeologist to toady to the academic community as it is to toady to the various review groups. The state archaeologist who does not constantly and fairly critique the products of the archaeological community is failing to serve it. To advance the cause of archaeology, the state archaeologist must earn the ire of other archaeologists.

Since the readers of this volume will be primarily archaeologists, I shall conclude with an admonition. Expect your state archaeologist to watch your work very closely, criticize your reports and often ignore your recommendations. State archaeologists frequently operate with more information on total projects and may not have the time to explain each individual decision. Asking for such explanations may lead to the destruction of even more sites as valuable time is taken from review and negotiation. The state archaeologist is certainly sympathetic to the goals of traditional archaeology but is also looking at cultural resources management from a much broader perspective. They are individuals of great dedication who are both the pathfinders and the rear guard in the fight to prevent the loss of archaeological resources. Yet, whatever a state archaeologist does, he is doomed to lose since the sites which are saved from the bulldozer are being saved for someone else to destroy in a "scientific" manner at a later date.

PROBLEMS IN THE ORGANIZATION AND GROWTH OF CORPORATE ARCHAEOLOGY[1]

William K. Macdonald
University of Michigan
Ann Arbor, Michigan

and

Alexander H. Townsend
National Heritage Corporation
West Chester, Pennsylvania

During the past several years the enactment and tentative enforcement of state and federal laws mandating archaeological investigation to provide for the proper treatment of prehistoric and historic cultural resources has been largely responsible for creating a situation in which large sums of money are available to those willing and, hopefully, qualified to undertake such investigations.[2] In response to the availability of money, an as yet undetermined number of new and preexisting profit-based organizations of all sizes have begun to offer archaeological services and compete for available contracts.

The purpose of this paper is to outline a number of problems inherent in the practice of what we label here as *corporate archaeology*: problems stemming from such considerations as competition, maximization of profits, research qualifications, contributions to pure research, and maintenance of adequate archaeological research standards.

Initially, however, it may be of value to define what we mean by corporate archaeology. While a number of terms are frequently used as synonyms for this term, we feel they are unsatisfactory for various reasons. Contract archaeology seems too inclusive, since much research is subsumable under this term, ranging from that done years ago under the auspices of the Works Progress Administration to that done for the National Science Foundation to anything done by someone under contract. Similarly, conservation archaeology includes work performed by the more traditional structures, such as university and museum excavations and surveys, and seems intended to define the purpose of research in relation to the cultural resources in question, e.g., environmental impact statements, salvage excavations, etc., rather than the organizational structures under which that research is carried out. On the other hand, corporate archaeology, defined here as the provision of archaeological research services by an organizational structure for financial gain, suggests the scope and purpose of what we are discussing and emphasizes those areas in which we will suggest that serious problems are most likely to arise.

It should come as no surprise to anyone that the primary purpose of any corporate venture is to show a profit but, since it seems so obvious, it is most likely to be forgotten. We would like to emphasize here that the primary and perhaps only reason that business is at present interested in archaeological research is that money is available for archaeology and the traditional structures--universities, state archaeological offices and museums--have been unable and perhaps unwilling to respond to this recently developing situation. Ironically, it was precisely the members of the traditional organizations who, lobbying vigorously for much needed legislation for the protection of cultural resources, created the present situation. Some archaeologists are quite awed by the monster that they have helped create.

Further, it should not be forgotten that the only reason this archaeology is being paid for is because it is required by both state and federal law. Aside from such agencies as the National Park Service, which has had a long involvement in archaeology, it is almost certain that though many contracting agencies, which are the clients of corporate archaeologists, are now handling large sums of money for archaeology, they would not contract for such services were it not required. It should be presumed that power companies and the like would get out of the business of contracting archaeology as quickly as laws requiring it were repealed. This is, of course, patently manifest in the system of competitive bidding which characterizes the awarding of many contracts for archaeological research services.

The implications of legal sanctions and competitive bidding for archaeological research are enormous and, moreover, they are in the long run deleterious to meaningful archaeological research. A situation in which an unwilling client contracts for undesired work to a company which owes its continued existence to pleasing that client is a clear case of conflict of interest when dealing with a public trust. We note again that the corporate archaeologist is involved in a profit-based enterprise; the business *must* show a profit which requires that he serve the interests of the client. Conflict with the client is dangerous to the continuance of corporate existence.

Most of us are aware that archaeology is presently experiencing a job-depressed condition. This situation seems to be the result of the ambitious expansion of graduate departments of anthropology during the 1960s and is probably a situation that will continue for a number of years. A number of these recent graduates are competing for jobs not only in the areas of traditional archaeological employment but also the corporate sphere. It is apparent, however, that the corporate world is less than competent to determine the range of archaeologists' abilities, with respect to the management of cultural resources since they have dealt less with them than have the traditional structures. Most business executives are not qualified to recognize a competent archaeologist. Most corporations, it seems likely, hire an archaeologist on the basis of his degree and reputation of his university (which looks good in a company brochure) or to meet affirmative action criteria. It is also apparent that few corporations realize the nature of archaeology as a discipline. The belated recognition by archaeologists that "nobody understands us," it should be noted, is a direct result of the failure of the discipline in its responsibility as an educational profession. Fortunately, there are signs that this is changing: one archaeologist we know has been teaching archaeological principles to grammar school students, and the state archaeological program in Arkansas has publicized similar public-oriented efforts.

The result of this lack of appreciation of the nature of archaeology by corporations that hire archaeologists, by the public whom archaeologists supposedly serve, and especially by the clients who pay for archaeological research, is a highly probable reduction in the quality of archaeology undertaken within the corporate sphere. It is presumably to prevent this probability that certification measures are being worked out to be imposed on the discipline. In other words, the members of the traditional structures are scrambling to prevent the logical consequences of their own actions.

The individual archaeologist conducting research within a corporate structure is, in fact, faced with the task of attempting to maximize three separate goals: profit, client satisfaction, and research standards. This, of course, places the archaeologist in the logically and pragmatically inconsistent position of 1) attempting to satisfy a client who is, in turn, attempting to maximize the returns of his investment (i.e., the archaeologist must give the most for the least amount of money); 2) attempting to satisfy his employer who is, of necessity, concerned with profit maximization (i.e., the archaeologist must hold nonchargeable man-hours expended to a minimum); and 3) attempting to satisfy himself through the maximization of research standards. This latter condition assumes, perhaps unrealistically, that corporate archaeologists are capable of formulating a mazeway that requires high standards of research. Ideally, attempts should be made to maximize all three of the above goals, but the most likely effects of this triadic situation is the lowering of the overall quality of research.

The pitfalls of the corporate archaeologist can be briefly visualized as a flowchart which outlines a hierarchy of project survival levels (Figure 1). This flowchart presents a somewhat pessimistic overview of the processes involved in attempting to complete an archaeological project in a corporate setting. It is, on the other hand, an accurate reflection of more than a half dozen combined years of experience dealing with this form of archaeology. Satisfaction, as noted in Figure 1, may be conceived of in varying terms--money and time are the most obvious--but the pressure is never, in our experience, to improve the quality of research design, unless by some quirk or accident it happens to bear on another aspect of the project.

Corporate Structures for Research

As indicated above, the manner in which corporate archaeology has developed suggests to us the probability that research standards will be lowered. This is a result not only of limitations on money and time, but stems from the physical prerequisites inherent in archaeological research. While archaeology is still an essentially labor-intensive discipline, advances in manipulative and curatorial requisites have established a need for multidisciplinary and sophisticated approaches to research. In order to continue to competently carry out archaeological research it is no longer adequate, if indeed it ever was, to supply a number of bodies with shovels or trowels and turn them loose on a gridded site. Therefore, it is apparent that in order to carry out competent research it is necessary to duplicate the range of services in the corporate sphere that is available to the university or museum. Soil and pollen

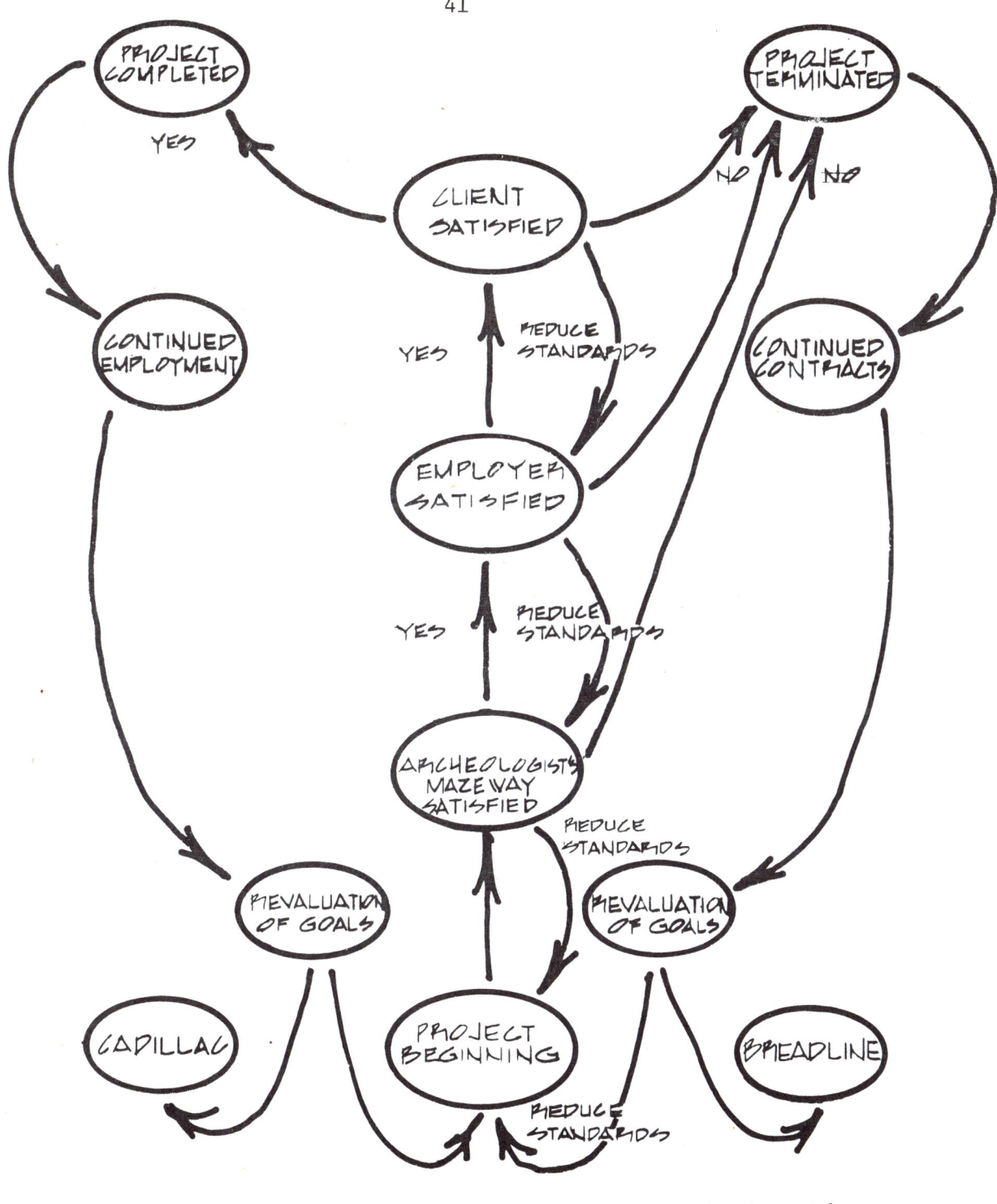

FIGURE 1: Contract projects flowchart showing pressures to reduce quality of archaeological research. In some cases archaeologist and employer may be the same individual; the pressures, however, remain the same, as do the probable results.

analysis, artifact analysis and conservation, large-scale coding and cataloging of materials recovered and observed are now, and should remain, an integral and important part of our work as archaeologists. Physico-chemical analytical techniques such as neutron activation, thermoluminescence, trace element analysis and various computer-oriented analytical studies are generally available within a university setting. Thus, the question arises: Can corporate archaeology duplicate such services while remaining within the strictures of profit maximization and client satisfaction? Additionally: Are contracting agencies willing--or even able--to comprehend the absolute necessity of such analysis in order to maintain what should be minimal standards of research? Obviously not every one of these techniques is applicable to every project but it is clear, we think, that they should exist as options which may be chosen by the archaeologist within the context of his research design.

Obviously, a company must reduce the number of idle hours among its employees in order to lower payroll and overhead burden. In order to accomplish this it may be necessary to utilize archaeological personnel in nonarchaeological activities during periods when archaeological projects are unavailable. In this regard it may be of interest to note that, in general, university archaeologists are professional teachers, museum archaeologists are professional curators, conservators and public tutors, and state archaeologists are professional coordinators or, more frequently, public relations personnel and lobbyists. Each of these types of archaeologist has a primary mode of livelihood other than a strictly archaeological one. Corporate archaeologists, on the other hand, are most likely to be unemployed if archaeological projects are unavailable in sufficient quantity to economically justify their existence within a profit oriented structure. This may be the cause of no little amount of job anxiety and may lead to the further reduction of research standards unless any dead time can be economically accounted for.

A further consideration is worthy of discussion at this point; that is, the existence of profit potential and the necessity to make a living may encourage the side-stepping of research qualifications. In other words, the corporate archaeologist, in an attempt to maximize profits or simply in an attempt to keep his job, may begin competing for contracts for archaeological services which he and/or his company are not fully qualified to provide. The time has long passed when archaeology was a small discipline in which participants could stumble across temporal and spatial boundaries with the same set of techniques and perspectives. Historical archaeologists, in particular, are aware, we think, of what can be done to an historic site if the investigator is unfamiliar with the data base and the technical requirements of such a site. The importance of such an attitude lies in the implied assumption which it makes--the corporate structure assumes the inherent similarity of all sites and periods. We feel quite certain that in order to attempt to do justice to the entire range of archaeological data in this country a corporation would need an inordinately large staff of archaeologists which would in turn be strongly counterproductive to the maximization of profit potential. Even within the segment of archaeology which has been designated historical, the diversity of problems and data are such that we doubt that a single archaeologist could be considered competent in all areas.

From this discussion we suggest that corporate structures for archaeological research must, because of its nature, either specialize to the possible extent of severely restricting the range of available contracts, or become so large as to make the maintenance of such structures for research economically disastrous. For reasons noted below, we feel that the first of these alternatives is the only realistic solution to the maximization of research, client satisfaction and, possibly, profit.

Present Status of Corporate Archaeology

It is difficult to assess the present status of corporate archaeology since we don't know exactly how many corporations or freelance individuals are involved in the field. Channels of communication have not yet developed between corporate archaeological structures, a phenomenon probably attributable, in large part, to increasing competition among such firms. Given increasing competition, moreover, the likelihood that information resulting from corporate archaeological research would be disseminated is probably nil. The lack of communication among corporate archaeologists has fragmented this segment of the discipline.

The fragmentation which presently characterizes corporate archaeology is at least partially responsible for the sanctions which have been considered for the discipline as a whole. The move to register and/or certify all practitioners of archaeology is an attempt to prevent incompetent and deleterious research and, whatever one's opinions about the methods proposed for accomplishing this laudable goal, the probable effect appears to us to be twofold: first, such procedures will probably result in protecting the niches of various archaeologists rather than providing for the protection of archaeological resources; and, second, such procedures seem bent on hindering corporations from obtaining contracts by requiring them to have facilities which they cannot provide with the stricture of profit.

The reaction of those involved in traditional archaeological research to the engagement of corporate structures in the practice of archaeology is interesting and will be of increasing importance to practitioners of corporate archaeology if present trends continue. Some states, for example, have adopted policies through permit-dispensing agencies of not allowing extralocal corporations to carry out research within their borders. Further, some museums and other public institutions have begun to assess corporate archaeologists fees for access to their resources.[3] We see these and similar reactions as harmful to the progress of all archaeological research, corporate or otherwise.

With these diverse and seemingly disconnected points in mind, the remainder of this paper will be devoted to a brief exploration of possible strategies by which corporate archaeologists can maximize potential within the context of the limiting conditions noted above.

Directions for Corporate Archaeology

In order to logically develop the argument outlined below it is necessary to state explicitly a number of premises upon which this argument is based. We do this as a matter of convenience and form primarily because there has been a great amount of discussion of these points recently and the argument we develop below makes little sense outside of this context.

First, archaeological sites and the objects contained therein are a public trust. This is, of course, an old tenet of the archaeological profession, but its inclusion here is a recognition of the ethical implications of deriving profit from the destruction of a public trust.

Second, the indiscriminate retrieval of data to "save it from destruction," i.e., salvage archaeology, is, in effect, the same thing as pot hunting. The increase in archaeological funding from governmental sources, as well as from business, in the form of legally required impact statements, historic preservation studies and cultural resource management planning has forced the discipline into an awareness that salvage as salvage is no longer a small and ignorable portion of the work being done. The shrinking of traditional funding sources has made this money, if not the work it entails, more desirable than ever before.

Third, sites are only of significance in relation to the problems for which they supply data; the notion that some sites are more important than others because of their relative temporal and/or spatial position is counterproductive to archaeological research. This holds true whether one's theoretical perspective is that of an historian or that of an anthropologist, scientific or otherwise.

These assumptions, in conjunction with the discussion presented above, lead us to the conclusion that no corporation can impartially dispense judgments on the value of one site over another. Without impartiality, or the pretense of it, the justification of corporate involvement in archaeological research becomes a chimera and nothing more. We, therefore, suggest that the only viable direction in which corporate archaeology may go is toward greater specialization and that the onus of responsibility for ethical judgments concerning the maintenance of a public trust should remain the province of the traditional structures of archaeological research which, removed from the strictures of profit and client satisfaction, may be expected to retain some degree of judicious impartiality.

It may be appropriate to include here the suggestion that one way in which the present disordered situation could be alleviated is by providing a general pool of funds from projects affected by such legislation as the Moss-Bennett bill to be used for support of research relative to the significance of the archaeological problems of a given area. If, for example, 1 percent of all construction budgets were diverted to a single fund under the administration of a centralized, nonprofit organization (a state archaeologist's office or a Park Service subregional office, for example) those funds could then be disbursed differentially on the basis of the worth of individual projects within the region in proportion to the amount of information contributed about the archaeology of that region. Such a program would function in a manner similar to traditional granting institutions, such as NSF, with the attendant and beneficial peer evaluation procedures. Further, this would reduce coordination problems inherent in a large number of surveys duplicating efforts in an area and would concentrate the efforts of workers in the area on more problem-oriented projects by maximizing the efficiency of fund use. The coherence of research programs would be greatly enhanced and, by removing the participation of corporate archaeologists from the area of impact statements, the inherent conflict of interest noted above would be considerably lessened. Such a system of funds disbursement should allow for a more unbiased series of judgments concerning the nature and amount of impact on the cultural resources of an area by deferring the judgment to a disinterested third party whose main concern is the archaeological resources of the area rather than the amount of return on an investment. This is but one of a number of possible suggestions for the resolution of some of the problems facing the discipline, but one which we have not seen elsewhere. We dislike the idea of a controlling registry or licensing board restricting research and it seems to us that the merits of recognizing differences in occupational interests within the discipline forces recognition not of levels of professionals, but of varieties of professionals, differentially competent in aspects of a growing discipline.

The question whether corporate archaeology should tend toward specialization rather than diversification is still open, however. If

we remove the corporate archaeologist--presumably kicking and screaming--
from the area of environmental impact statement research, what is left
for the corporate archaeologist to do?

Intuitively, we doubt that corporate archaeology can long survive
as an independent, profit-making venture. Our view is that the best a
corporation can hope to attain for its archaeology segment is the status
of a self-sustaining--as opposed to profit-making--unit within a structure
aimed at providing a larger range of services of which archaeology is an
integrated, though relatively minor, part. Alternatively, a corporation
could develop a service ancillary to the discipline as a whole: pollen
analysis, soil analysis, various physical, chemical and analytical
techniques could be used, much as various C-14 services, as the basis of
corporate profit. We think that the possibilities are enormous,
potentially profitable and of considerable importance to the development
of innovative techniques useful to the entire discipline.

Since we consider it unlikely that corporate archaeologists will
pay any attention whatsoever to anyone who suggests that their means
of livelihood is not going to continue much longer, we would like to
close this paper with a list of pollyanna suggestions for the consideration
of our colleagues:

First, as noted above, there are no channels of communication among
corporate archaeologists (although one possibility, dependent upon the
establishment of a registry, has been suggested by the Society for
American Archaeology). It would certainly be beneficial to be able to

obtain the results of research performed by other corporate archaeologists. This is probably the most inexcusable aspect of corporate archaeology--its failure to inform colleagues of the results of research.

Second, price-fixing is apparently illegal, but the practice of competitive bidding must somehow be stopped; seed money and loss-taking are practices which should be deplored. Perhaps it is asking too much of the disparate group which makes up corporate archaeology that it adhere to a code of ethics, but we doubt the ethical validity of underbids in excess of tens of thousands of dollars and more for a single project.

Third, since we should be able to recognize our corporate strengths and weaknesses relative to a research project, the possibility of subcontracting and joint projects seems feasible, even if not probable.

Finally, we are of the opinion that it is in our own best interest both as professionals and scholars to lobby vigorously for changes in the structure of traditional archaeological organizations.

NOTES

1. This paper is a revised version of a paper read at the symposium: Historical Archaeology as a Profession: Problems, Approaches, and Methods, 9th Annual Meeting of the Society for Historical Archaeology, 8 January, 1976, Philadelphia.

2. *Acknowledgments*: This paper has profited from discussions with members of the staff at National Heritage Corporation, especially John D. Milner, AIA, President. In addition, Macdonald has benefitted from lengthy discussions with Tom Riley, University of Illinois-Urbana, and Drs. Richard Ford and Karl Hutterer, University of Michigan. Advice was frequently given and less frequently taken, which is the fault of the authors, to whom all responsibility for error must accrue.

3. The need for users for curated materials in museums to support those structures is obvious. Museums, however, seem to have inconsistent and sometimes capricious policies which are rarely explicit. We don't mean to suggest that museums are specifically discriminating only against corporations, but simply that this may have deleterious consequences for the carrying out of individual projects.

THE ACQUISITION OF ARCHAEOLOGICAL CONTRACTS

Alex H. Townsend
National Heritage Corporation
West Chester, Pennsylvania

This paper is intended to make explicit the factors which must be taken into consideration in the search for, and in the pursuit and negotiation of research contracts by archaeologists. It is my own opinion, based upon experience in contract negotiations within a corporate environment, that these factors are best understood as a series of ordered decisions beginning with a search for potential contracts and ending (for the purposes of this paper) with contract negotiation. As discussed in the following paragraphs, contract acquisition is ultimately based upon individual ethical standards and further involves considerations of experience, research interests, financial gain, the promise of additional contracts, and more. For convenience, this discussion is divided into three sections, entitled Search, Pursuit, and Negotiation, each representing one stage in the procuring of archaeological contracts within a competitive market system.

Search

While probably the easiest phase of the process to discuss and the most readily understood, the importance of search activities should not be underestimated. Basic decisions relative to the stance one is to take in a service market must be made at this stage of contract acquisition. These choices will have the effect of limiting the kinds of contracts one can expect to secure.

The process of archaeological contract search involves a flow of information in two directions. Advertising one's archaeological capabilities and availability is the first of these information flows, the objective being to inform as many potential clients as possible of one's ability and willingness to accept research contracts. By whatever means this information is channeled, whether by letter, brochure, word of mouth, etc., some indication of specific research specialization and preference is also communicated to potential clients. This information shapes initial client reaction to a particular firm. Given that it is impossible in practice for any particular archaeological firm to offer all types of archaeological services for all types of archaeological sites in all areas of the United States, the communication of research specialities becomes an ethical necessity (see Macdonald and Townsend, this volume, for a discussion of this point). Advertising, in the broadest sense of the word, is the most effective and rewarding mode of contract search. My own experience suggests that a great majority of contracts are secured as a result of client-initiated negotiations. At the same time, the advertisement of research specializations has both negative as well as positive implications for contract acquisition. It serves not only to limit the types and number of contracts a firm is likely to be offered, but also to maximize acquisition of those types of contracts in which one is most interested.

Obviously, communication of research interests is effected by the specific information channeled to potential clients, as well as the selective distribution of that information. Initially one must decide which potential clients are to be informed of one's capabilities, which is, in fact, a decision as to who one's potential clients really are (a New England based firm, for example, would be ill advised to invest money advertising its services in California). Also involved is a decision regarding those particular capabilities or research interests one wishes to emphasize to potential clients. It may prove more profitable in terms of contract acquisition to emphasize research capabilities in archaeological survey in communications aimed at the Corps of Engineers, since most contracts administered by that agency involve field survey, while it is probably an advantage to emphasize capabilities in both excavation and survey to state and local level agencies.

The second mode of contract search is simply the reverse of the first, that is, attempting to keep informed of the needs of potential clients for archaeological research services. This involves the maintenance of verbal channels of communication with certain individuals and agencies, channels which may have been opened through advertising of services, as well as subscription to publications listing state or federal solicitations for contract services. Solicitations for federally administered contracts are listed each day in the *Commerce Business Daily,* published by the U.S. Department of Commerce. A typical archaeological contract advertisement is quoted below which serves as an example for much of the discussion to follow. Like most services contracted by the Corps of Engineers, the following advertisement is for survey/inventory and assessment of cultural resources within a prescribed area.

R -- INVENTORY AND ASSESSMENT OF ARCHAEOLOGICAL AND HISTORIC RESOURCES FOR AREAS OF PROPOSED DIKE AND REVETMENT CONSTRUCTION along the Mississippi River in Tennessee and Mississippi. Should resources eligible for nomination to the National Register of Historic Places be identified, a range of possible mitigatory plans together with spective cost estimates will be provided for each resource. The work shall be performed in two phases. The first phase encompasses some 29 acres and the report on this work shall be required by 1 Aug 76. The second phase includes some 92 acres and the report shall be due 1 Jun 77. Some additional areas within the same general geographic area may be added during the contract life. Significant evaluation factors: availability of professional personnel, particularly those experienced in the states of Tennessee and Mississippi.

The work on the above four items, will be at a firm fixed price for all items scheduled at the time of contract negotiation. The contracts are expected to be awarded in late June 76. Interested firms considered must have two archaeologists and a historian with prior experience in research, field investigations and assessment of archaeological and historic sites. Significant evaluation factors and relative order of importance are: first, availability of professional personnel, particularly those experienced in the study of cultural resources in the state where project is located; second, to have adequate supporting personnel, such as field and laboratory technicians; and third, geographic location of the firm. Other significant evaluation factors are the additional considerations of the Department of Defense policy for selection. Firms having a current SF 251, U. S. Government Architect-Engineer Questionnaire, or SF 254, Architect-Engineer and Related Services Questionnaire, on file with the

> office shown below and those responding to
> these announcements before 25 May 76 with
> a completed SF 254 will be considered for
> selection. This is not a request for
> proposals. (*Commerce Business Daily*,
> May 12, 1976:6).

It may be profitable to examine this announcement in some detail in order to illustrate those factors which must be considered prior to the pursuit of a particular contract.

Contracted services in this case are presumably intended to provide for the proper treatment and recording of cultural resources (meaning prehistoric and historic sites) prior to the destruction of such resources by river control related construction. Accordingly, the solicitation states that two archaeologists and one historian, all with prior experience in the state involved, plus adequate laboratory and field support personnel, are required for consideration. Additional considerations are geographic location and familiarity with the criteria for nomination to the National Register of Historic Places. Finally, the solicitation states that "other significant evaluation factors are the additional considerations of the Department of Defense policy for selection," one such consideration being that of price.

But even assuming complete satisfaction of the stated requirements, certain practical and ethical points must be given consideration before one responds to the solicitation. First, and most obvious, is the consideration of proper treatment of any possible cultural resources in the project area--do the terms of the solicitation allow for such treatment? Time considerations alone make the proper treatment of resources difficult, at best. A period of one month between award of contract and submission of a final report is not a realistically adequate period for the stated research, and one must assume that the short period specified is necessitated by the scheduled start of construction. This, in turn, brings up yet another point for consideration--what is client reaction to proposed treatment of cultural resources likely to be in the face of a tight schedule for construction? For business purposes, the contract archaeologist must be concerned with client satisfaction in order to provide for the possibility of future contracts. Further, the solicitation states that only sites eligible for nomination to the National Register of Historic Places will be the subject of possible salvage excavation. While the criteria for nomination of archaeological sites are quite broad, nomination does not lead invariably to placement on the Register. Much difficulty was experienced, for example, by those who were finally successful in having the largest Indian mound in the United States, at Cahokia, Illinois, placed on the National Register.

On a more practical basis, business considerations involve such problems as profit, the prospect of additional contracts, and enough overhead to cover time spent on preparing a proposal. Obviously, any business is concerned with profit, and the business of archaeology is no exception. Profit allows for growth and expansion, coverage of dead time, etc., all factors of importance to contract archaeologists. A one month contract, however, does not generally return a profit when proposal costs are high. Since such costs are not reimbursable, one is then forced to rely upon the possibility of additional contracts to erase any loss which results from a small initial contract. Occasionally, however, a decision may be made to accept a loss on a particular project in order to gain familiarity ("get a foot in the door") with a potential major client (such as the Corps of Engineers), again banking upon the possibility of additional contracts.

All of these factors and more (scheduling of personnel, potential competition, etc.) must be taken into consideration before a decision is made to pursue a particular contract. Assuming, however, that all ethical and practical misgivings are overcome or, at least, one is interested in obtaining more information about the project before making a final decision as to its merits, acquisition then moves to the stage of Pursuit. It is quite impossible to determine whether or not ethical responsibilities for the treatment of cultural resources can be satisfied on the basis of incomplete information about the project area in the cited example.

Pursuit

By whatever means knowledge of a potential contract is gained, then, the first major decision must be one of whether or not to pursue, usually made on the basis of very little information about the site, about client motivation, or about the amount of money available. Generally, very little time is available for submission of an initial response to a solicitation--thirteen days in the case of the example given above--which does not allow much time for a consideration of necessary variables, and can result in the submission of unqualified responses by contract archaeologists.

A response to a contract solicitation, however, may be followed by an invitation to submit a proposal. An invitation of this kind is usually accompanied by additional information about the site, which allows, if nothing else, a more judicious appraisal of the potential contract on the basis of the considerations given above. With such additional information it should be possible to determine, for example, whether a period of one month is sufficient to allow an adequate treatment of potential resources in the area covered by phase one of the solicitation quoted earlier. Some indication may also be gained concerning the amount of money the client wishes to spend. Available money is always of extreme importance in the consideration of any potential contract as money translates directly into time. All of the practical and ethical considerations outlined under Contract Search must now be reconsidered in the light of new information and a decision made as to whether or not to submit a formal proposal in further pursuit of the contract.

Based upon an estimate of what the client is willing to spend, then, a preliminary proposal for professional services is drawn up, including an explicit statement of the scope of the services, time allocation, responsibilities of the archaeologist, client responsibilities, and a cost breakdown. While it is usually the case that a proposal is not accepted at face value by the client, the proposal nevertheless represents a statement by the archaeologist of his understanding of a particular project and the manner in which he feels it should best be carried out (given the time and money available).

The scope of services to be performed is really the heart of a proposal and should be expressed in the form of archaeological goals, client goals, use to which the resulting information is to be put, research interests, etc. This provides all concerned with a standard against which project success can be measured following completion of a final report. Research interests of the archaeologist should be included or reflected in the project goals, but it seems important to avoid giving the client an impression that he is paying additional monies solely for the satisfaction of the archaeologist's own interests--research interests should be consistent with the overall project design. It serves no real purpose to submit a formal proposal which, in the mind of the archaeologist, contrasts sharply with the position of the client. This results in either a simple rejection of the proposal or a lengthy negotiation and rewriting which can cause spiraling proposal costs.

A statement of responsibilities for both parties to the contract is also an important part of any proposal. For the archaeologist, this will involve report deadlines, submission of progress reports, disposition of artifactual material, ownership of photographic and other records, etc. It should be specified, for example, that artifacts and photographic negatives are to be returned to the client for disposition to a proper archival repository after a given period of time. For the client, on the other hand, it is absolutely essential that a statement authorizing access to any and all available and applicable resource material be included within the contract. While it may be difficult in particular instances for a client to determine exactly what information the archaeologist desires, it is nevertheless important to agree beforehand upon a policy permitting access to resource material, preferably before the actual field investigations begin. Additionally, client responsibilities may include such considerations as the provision of additional labor and/or machinery for excavation if needed, on-site consultation, and labor for backfilling of excavations.

A sufficient amount of project funds must also be allocated for reimbursable expenses, which include such items as travel (air fares, car rental, mileage charges, etc.), subsistence, photographic supplies, miscellaneous field expenses, printing and graphics, equipment rental, etc. Estimates for reimbursable expenses should be realistic as cost overruns in expenses are subtracted directly from profits and overhead.

If a cost breakdown is required by the client, then the hours to be spent on a project should be divided between field investigations, laboratory analysis, and report preparation. Many clients, however, are not totally convinced of the necessity for a thorough artifact analysis as a necessary part of archaeological investigation. In such cases it may be easier, in terms of proposal acceptance, to divide project hours into two parts--the first being for field investigation and the second for artifact analysis and report preparation--lumping analysis and report preparation into a single block of hours. It is generally possible in this manner to allocate at least fifty percent of project time to analysis and report preparation, obviously less than ideal but, in most cases, a workable allocation.

The expenditure of time and money proposed by the archaeologist will represent a compromise between what he sees as an ideal allocation and what he would be willing to accept as a minimum condition for acceptance of the contract. Only rarely are the conditions seen as ideal by the archaeologist acceptable to the client, but the archaeologist must nevertheless establish a figure for the number of hours necessary to satisfactorily complete a particular project in terms of project scope and proper treatment of a cultural resource. If it seems likely at this point that the client is either unwilling or unable to meet this minimum figure, a decision must be made whether or not to submit a formal proposal. Acceptance of a figure below that which the archaeologist sees as a minimum for proper treatment of the cultural resource in questions, without an agreed upon reduction in project scope, will likely result in either an improper treatment of the resource or a cost overrun, neither of which the contract archaeologist can afford. If, however, the archaeologist is satisfied that the client will fund sufficient research to satisfy project goals, that he himself is capable of satisfying project goals, that the project is economically feasible (in terms of either immediate or long-range profit potential), that his chances for securing the contract are good in the face of competition, then the proposal is formalized and submitted to the potential client. Following a review by the client the proposal either is rejected or the archaeologist is contracted for negotiation of a final contract.

Negotiation

A decision to enter into negotiation with a particular archaeologist or his firm represents a commitment on the part of the client toward an acceptance of the position put forth in the proposal by that archaeologist or firm. At the simplest level this may merely consist of a complete acceptance of a proposal by the client and the signing of a final contract with an authorization to begin field investigations on a certain date. Contract negotiation, however, is rarely quite this easy.

It should not be presumed that contract negotiation is concerned solely with the proposed fee, though this is generally a principal factor. A knowledgeable client, such as the National Park Service, is equally concerned with a mutual agreement regarding project scope, and will endeavor to ensure a full understanding of project needs on the part of the archaeologist through a clarification of specific goals.

This further emphasizes the need for a well written proposal, containing statements of client needs and goals, which has as its first reward an amelioration or shortening of the negotiation process. The proposal of a reasonable and somewhat flexible price will obviously have a similar effect upon negotations.

In those cases where excavation and report submission schedules have not been specified in advance by the client, such scheduling will also become a consideration during negotiations. While these dates will be determined in part by project funding and the client's need for information, the archaeologist should insist upon a comfortable date for report submission. Where client need for information is acute and the archaeologist is pressed for an early submission, it may be possible to extend the report deadline through an agreement permitting either a preliminary report at the completion of field investigations or a series of bi-weekly reports during the course of excavation. This latter strategy has the additional benefit of providing a channel for client feedback during the investigations, thus allowing the client to suggest modifications in project scope, goals, methods and strategy, as he feels such modifications will result in a maximization of goal satisfaction.

As indicated above, negotiation almost always involves a discussion of the proposed fee and a knowledge of the considerations which are involved in reaching a mutual agreement on price is thus critical for an understanding of negotiation. These considerations can perhaps best be understood in terms of upper and lower limits for project price.

First, and most obvious, the upper limit for project price is set by the very real budget limitations of the client and, where these limitations are understood by the archaeologist, he is in a better position to propose a realistic price or to propose modifications in project scope to fit available monies. The archaeologist is not always made aware of budget limitations, one example being the solicitation quoted earlier, in which case he has no alternative but to propose a price based solely upon his understanding of project scope and the amount of work he feels is necessary for goal satisfaction and proper treatment of the cultural resources in question. There exists every possibility, however, that a price proposed in the absence of knowledge regarding client budget restrictions will greatly lengthen the amount of time and effort expended in contract negotiation, having the effect of reducing or even erasing project profits.

On the other hand, it is the archaeologist, not the client, who should be responsible for determining the lower price limitation for acceptance of a contract. The actual determination of a minimum price will involve a large number of factors, some of which are discussed below, but it is important to stress that the archaeologist bears the responsibility for its determination and, should all attempts to reach a mutually agreeable price fail, he has the final option to reject the contract entirely. Such rejection is done only as a last resort, but is preferable nonetheless to an acceptance resulting in cost overruns or a failure to satisfy project goals due to time limitations.

Those factors which the archaeologist should consider in his determination of minimum price are those which have been stressed throughout this paper. The archaeologist is responsible for ensuring the proper treatment of the cultural resources at hand, he is likewise responsible for the satisfaction of project goals, and will in most cases be concerned with the satisfaction of personal research goals as well. This latter concern reflects the level of interest the archaeologist has in a particular project and may result in his acceptance of a minimal price.

As discussed in an earlier section, the contract archaeologist is dependent upon profit for continued existence in a competitive service market, although he may be willing to forego a profit under certain circumstances, usually with an expectation of securing more profitable contracts in future negotiations. This strategy, however, may have an adverse effect upon future negotiations, as the client is liable to plan allocations for contract archaeological services using the cost breakdown contained in the original contract as a guide. In other words, the archaeologist may only be establishing a precedent of low-priced services with the client, a precedent which may be difficult to overcome in future negotiations.

The client, then, attempts to maximize returns on his investment, in terms of information retrieved (except in those cases where a client is funding research only because that research is required by law, and the final report is to be used only as an exhibit of compliance), by insisting upon a maximum of service at a minimum of price, while the archaeologist attempts to maximize research and profits. Where both client and archaeologist are in agreement on the maximization of information retrieval, and the archaeologist has submitted a proposal incorporating some amount of price flexibility, a mutual agreement on project price is generally a matter of simple negotiation. Where the client is interested only in the satisfaction of legal requirements and the archaeologist is concerned primarily with profit, negotiations are likely to be lengthy and expensive. Whatever the nature and length of price negotiations, the result should be a price agreeable to both parties--the client satisfied with the amount of research he will get in return for his investment, and the archaeologist satisfied that he can perform the work in accordance with professional and ethical standards and at a profit. The final price will be somewhere between the financial limitations of the client and the financial needs of the archaeologist.

In sum, the goal of contract negotiation is the securing of a research contract with the prospect of an immediate or future profit, a contract which (based upon all available information) will provide not only financial reward but which will also provide proper treatment of cultural resources, satisfaction of client needs, data for the archaeologist's own research interests, etc. Negotiation should ensure a mutual agreement on project scope and goals, an understanding of mutual responsibilities, and a realistic price for the agreed services. If both parties are satisfied that these conditions have been met, then the contract is finalized and signed and the process of contract acquisition is complete.

Conclusion

It was stated in the introduction that the purpose of this paper is to make explicit those ethical and practical considerations involved in the search, pursuit and negotiation of archaeological contracts, and that these considerations are best seen within the perspective of a series of decisions for contract acquisition which can now be diagrammed as a decision model (Figure 2). At every stage of contract acquisition a decision must be made by the archaeologist, based upon ethical and practical considerations, whether to continue the acquisition process for a particular contract.

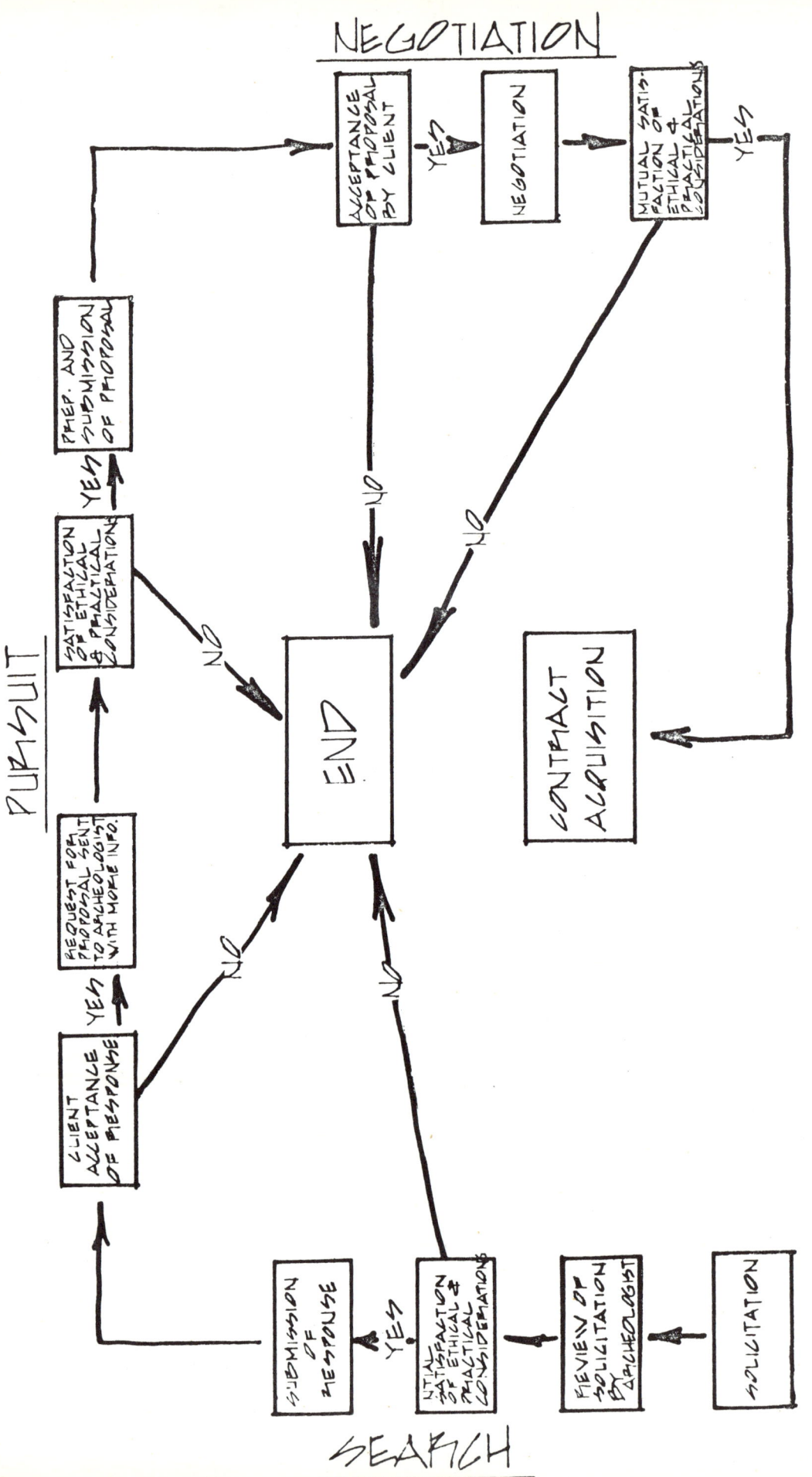

Figure 2: A simplified diagram illustrating the stages and steps comprising the process of contract acquisition. Note the occurrence of ethical and practical considerations at each stage, the failure to satisfy these conditions resulting in a termination of the acquisition process.

Most of the factors involved in contract acquisition decisions must be considered anew in the light of additional information at each stage of the process, although the importance of any particular factor may vary from one stage to the next. These factors which must be considered in contract search, for example, include considerations of research qualifications, the proper treatment of archaeological resources, client motivation and probable reaction to research results, the likelihood for future contracts, and potential competition, among others. Research qualifications and the proper treatment of the subject resources are the more important considerations, however, simply because the amount of available information regarding a particular contract at this point may be quite small. Two additional factors, the identification of potential clients and the differential distribution of information regarding research specialization and qualifications are important only in contract search and do not represent factors for consideration in contract pursuit and negotiation.

In contract pursuit, which really involves the formulation of a statement by the archaeologist as to his understanding of a project and the manner in which he feels it should be carried out, client motivation and prospects for profit begin to play a more important role as factors for consideration, in addition to a more realistic consideration of the treatment of cultural resources. As mentioned earlier, the scope of services and appropriate fee proposed at this stage will have a significant effect upon subsequent negotiations by either shortening or lengthening the time expended in formulating a mutually agreeable contract.

The proper treatment and recording of cultural resources continues to be an extremely important consideration during the stage of negotiation, as it was during contract search and pursuit. Considerations of financial gain also assume major proportions as the client strives to maximize returns on his investment and the archaeologist attempts to maximize profits. It is important to stress once again that it is the responsibility of the archaeologist to establish a price limit below which the conditions of the contract, as understood and set forth in a proposal, cannot be satisfied without a cost overrun. If the negotiated price falls below this minimum level, acceptance of the contract would occur only with a strong prospect of future profits.

In conclusion, most of the factors discussed in this paper must be considered at each stage of contract acquisition, the result of this consideration being a decision whether or not to continue the acquisition process or to search for another possible contract. If one factor were singled out as most important it would without question be the treatment of archaeological or cultural resources which form the focus of any particular research project. Treatment of cultural resources thus forms a thread of continuity throughout the stages of search, pursuit and negotiation, with the archaeologist's continued participation in contract acquisition hinging upon what he believes the proper treatment of particular resources to be, coupled with an insistence upon a contractual agreement ensuring that such treatment is allowed. This is not to deny that the goal of contract search, pursuit and negotiation is the acquisition of contracts in a competitive market, but is intended rather to emphasize that minimum price, project scope and goals, qualifications, satisfaction of client needs, etc., are all based upon the archaeologist's understanding of what constitutes a proper treatment of cultural resources.

CONTRACT ARCHAEOLOGY FROM THE OUTSIDE

Steven A. LeBlanc
Institute of Archaeology
University of California
Los Angeles, California

It is the intent of this paper to present a rather personal evaluation of contract archaeology in the United States. A certain distance from contract work can be claimed, as I have never participated in any contract work. However, much of the archaeological data relevant to my current research is the result of contract work, and I am certainly engaged in considerable "salvage" archaeology at the present in the sense that I am working on sites that are about to be destroyed and all data lost (LeBlanc 1975). Thus, both the needs and the results of contract work are very much in evidence from my perspective.

It is perhaps relevant to consider the distinction between contract and salvage archaeology. Although one sometimes feels the word contract is now in vogue because of the stigma associated with salvage work, it does seem more appropriate. The term contract seems to be used to refer to the means of funding work, while salvage unfortunately carries the connotation that the only means of mitigation is digging.

However, it is clear that both these terms almost universally refer to work on sites or areas that are chosen not by the archaeologist but by agents outside his control (e.g., government and other organizations). It is the nonselective aspect of this work, regardless of what it is called, that is at issue. While the term contract archaeology seems more appropriate, the underlying problems have not been removed by a name change.

It is the intent here to consider several problems involved in contract work, and to suggest some possible solutions. The most important goal will be to show that these problems seem solvable and that it is the responsibility of all archaeologists to see that such solutions are found. It is my contention that contract work as frequently practiced suffers from five major problems. These difficulties have very serious long-term consequences that must be considered and soon resolved.

Research Design and the Regional Approach

Due to the nature of most contract projects, the scope of analysis is different from what might be considered optimal. One reason is because this scope is usually too small. It has become increasingly clear that site-oriented research is not capable of providing the kinds of information that many archaeologists now consider essential. The analysis of particular sites must be integrated into a framework that includes the cultural system of which the site is a part and the general environmental background of the area. The development of such a framework usually involves the analysis of several sites or occupations in order to provide some temporal-spatial variability. The combination of excavation and survey and the sampling of several sites instead of the total excavation of a single site are obvious trends in the direction of providing a basis for a more regional synthesis.

From the analytic point of view, a regional, multisite approach is very much to be desired since archaeology's greatest tool is comparison. The ability to compare contemporary sites in different settings and nearby sites from different periods provides us with some of our most powerful analytic tools.

In some cases, then, contract work, by being restricted to a road right of way or other such arbitrary area, is hopelessly limited when compared to a proper regional study. In other cases, such as reservoir projects or strip mining projects, the problem areas may be large enough to provide a regional basis for analysis. In such cases contract work may be a blessing because such projects may be one of the few ways to provide sufficient funds to do proper regional studies. In fact, some very significant studies are precisely of this origin (e.g., Dittert, *et al.* 1961).

Unfortunately, institutions such as the National Park Service which are in a position to do good regional archaeology have failed to implement this need. None of the parks or monuments with which I am familiar have an overall research design. Where several sites are excavated, it is usually done sequentially with each site getting a descriptive report, and little or no comparative or regional analysis is done concurrent with the excavation.

Regardless of the potential for some regional contract projects, it would seem that the vast majority of contract projects are too small to be regionally oriented. The solution is obvious, but not practical:

Carry out regional work around each such limited project. Due to funding considerations this is, in most cases, impossible. However, it is entirely possible that for certain areas the known potential for considerable contract work over a number of years could make the design of a regional study practical and each project could be fitted into this design. Thus, for example, at essentially no cost one could have a graduate seminar design a regional study for an area known to be heavily impacted. With this design as a guide, archaeology done in the area could be related to this design over a five to ten year period. While obviously the implementation of such an effort is not trivial and one would want to make sure such a procedure did not result in fieldwork turning into a "cookbook" procedure, such an approach seems feasible given the proper motivation.

This suggestion, as others that follow, clearly calls for cooperation between academic and contract archaeologists. The trend toward separation between these two is noticeable both by the formation of contracting companies and the establishment of independent offices of contract work in academic settings. While the latter are an obvious result of the need for administrative coordination and, if properly executed, provide no threat to cooperation with academia, the potential is obviously present for further separation of the two "camps." The Park Service's attempt to locate archaeological staffs near universities is an encouraging sign of cooperation, although direct evidence of intellectual interaction is less obvious.

In sum, efforts must be made to imbed small scale contract projects into larger research designs. The solution involves close cooperation with academic archaeologists and seems potentially solvable if sufficient concern is given to the problem.

Local Expertise

Archaeology has long embraced within it two opposing elements: "old timers" who knew a particular data base intimately, and "outsiders" with diverse backgrounds and new approaches. Clearly the profession can profitably use both types. In order to do good archaeology one must eventually become an "old timer." Anyone who has worked in an area for a few months or especially a few years can look back with amazement at their naivete and lack of expertise concerning the local situation. Successful archaeology, whether one is an old timer or an outsider, requires doing one's homework and this consists of not only knowing the literature but dealing with the actual data and on-the-ground particulars.

It would seem that contract work decreases the possibility of being an old timer. Brief projects scattered over wide areas are all too common. It is a rare project in which three or four seasons are spent in the same general area. It seems that considerable insight is being lost in this process of hit and run archaeology. As various institutions begin to compete for the same projects, and hence cover increasingly larger areas, we must conclude that this process is accelerating.

Again, the solution is not obvious. One can only suggest that the use of consultants who really are specialists in an area would be an important step in the right direction. These specialists would probably be university or museum staff and this would also provide a means of encouraging cooperation between contractors and academia where it does not already exist. Thus, while the actual work may be done by junior people, senior specialists should be encouraged and expected to play an advisory role in the process. Contract work would benefit if the hiring of specialist-consultants became a standard practice.

Innovation

While the above considerations are by no means original, there is an important factor in contract work which is infrequently considered. Can contract work contribute to archaeology as a method? What roles does it and will it play in the development of new techniques, equipment, and procedures? Like all sciences, archaeology makes advances, in part, by improvements in hardware. The use of C-14, obsidian hydration, archaeomagnetic dating, flotation, remote sensing, etc., are methods that have greatly advanced our ability to collect the data we need. Less obviously, analytic methods such as cluster analysis, locational analysis, edge-wear studies, etc., and computer usage in general also contrubute to our ability to find out what we want to know.

It is not clear that contract work with its budgetary restrictions and its hurry up attitude will provide the millieu to generate or initially test such important innovations. While there may be ample funds for traditional, obviously needed efforts, contracts seem to provide few means to try a new technique (either in the field or laboratory) the results of which cannot be guaranteed. While a split between basic and applied work occurs in many disciplines, the rapidly changing role of "contract" and "research" archaeology is disturbing. If present trends continue, most archaeology will soon be contract work and most young archaeologists will be doing such jobs. If we are all applied, we will not progress. Again, the only presently practical solution is to keep contract work integrated into the discipline as a whole and to allow and encourage innovation and to discourage "standard" or rote efforts. It may mean that funding by NSF or other such agencies for certain aspects of contract work will become appropriate. Efforts will be needed to convince clients that "uncommon" archaeology is the type commonly done.

Artifact Storage

There is another most serious deficiency in some contract work that must be corrected very soon which has to do with the disposition of recovered artifacts. A basic rationale for contract work is that it preserves the archaeological record. Of course, this is not totally true. It has been repeatedly demonstrated that no archaeological effort preserves all the potential data from a site or that no more than a small part of such data is ever actually published.

I take it as a basic premise that all archaeology should be as problem-oriented as possible since this is the primary means to ensure that progress is made in solving questions at hand. Nevertheless, one must admit that not all archaeology, and especially not all contract archaeology, can hope to be totally problem-oriented; some pure description and inductive raw data collection must also occur.

While it is true that not all data can be collected from a site, with diligence, a great quantity can be gathered. Even if questions are not presently formulated concerning this body of data, it lies available for potential future reanalysis (see Clarke 1972 for a superb example of reanalysis). Thus, we might agree that the salvaging of a small site may mean little in itself, but when the region is studied some years later, data from such a site will be available for integration into a regional synthesis.

While reality is not quite as glowing as this line of reasoning would make it appear, there is nevertheless some validity to the above motivation to do contract work. Most archaeologists would agree that the majority of the data that exist after digging are intimately associated with the recovered artifacts. If these are discarded after analysis the purpose of the salvage is ignored. Who can believe that researchers even a decade or two hence will analyze artifactual material in the same way that it is done for the average contract report today?

Clearly, the very rationale of most contract work requires that all the material that is deemed worthy of collection today should be saved for future reanalysis. Yet a number of the most prestigious institutions engaged in contract work routinely discard all but a "representative" sample of the artifacts the public provided funds to save for posterity. This activity will in the future undoubtedly be viewed as a breach of the public trust.

The problem is not trivial. Storage space is at a premium at most institutions. However, as Lipe (1974) has pointed out, the cost of access to stored artifacts should be on the future user, so that high cost, easy access storage is not required. If even one percent of the funds of contract work were earmarked to cover the custodial duties performed by a designated institution, the use of some type of storehouse not necessarily on campus or easily accessible would provide a far better solution to this problem than the city dump.

Publication

Publication of archaeological data serves several purposes. It is the primary means of disseminating knowledge about what has been learned; and it also provides a means of passing on knowledge about how to do archaeology. Many small innovations, and occasionally large ones, do not enter the general repertoire of archaeology via specialized papers. Instead, they are brought to light as parts of data-oriented reports. Additionally, publications are read and reviewed by one's colleagues, which in all sciences provides the means for critical evaluation. This is perhaps a carrot-and-stick method of maintaining and advancing professional work, but it works.

Contract archaeology has not participated in this aspect of archaeology to any great extent. A great number of reports are never published, but are simply put on file with the appropriate agency. Others are published but in very obscure formats which are never advertised or widely disseminated, and certainly do not reach even the major university libraries. The proportion of contract sponsored projects that actually undergoes peer review is exceedingly small. Not only does this defeat one of the goals of contract work, but it certainly does not encourage high standards of work. If reports are not integrated into the general body of knowledge, they do not preserve the archaeological record.

It is true, of course, that many agencies have taken considerable steps to remedy this situation. It would not be difficult, however, to devote a few pages of *American Antiquity* or some other broadly circulated journal to a listing of the titles of all contract reports. This trivially easy step would make access to such reports markedly easier and would go a long way towards keeping contract work within the scholarly fold.

The stipulation that this be done as part of fulfilling a contract and that this be considered as one of the canons of the profession would ensure the compliance necessary to make this effort really useful. While such a step would have important benefits, full publication of all contract work should remain the long-term goal.

Implications for Archaeology

Given the above considerations, it seems that contract archaeology may not be contributing to the overall advancement of archaeology. The level of analysis and synthesis in archaeological reporting does not seem to be continuing to improve at the rate it did during the 1960s and there

seems to be an increasing amount of purely descriptive work. It may be
that the increased amount of contract work is having a stagnating effect
on the discipline. Regardless of the present effects on the discipline,
the impact of contract work on American archaeology is potentially
enormous and far reaching, and continued evaluation of its impact is
very important.

Of much less obvious import, but probably as significant, is the
effect of contract work on our public image. A major consideration is
whether the public is paying for something that they are not getting.
At present the general public has a great intrinsic interest in archaeology.
They have been told that contract work is saving for posterity priceless,
irreplaceable information concerning man's past. Yet all too often this
does not seem to be the case. A poorly analyzed, descriptive site report
and the saving of a "sample" of artifacts from a site is not the same as
saving man's past for posterity. When the public finally becomes aware
of this discrepancy, the disenchantment with archaeology may be severe.
We are now approaching the time when a national antiquities act might
come into being. If we cannot properly carry out the job presently
given us, then there seems little chance such an act will ever be realized.
Not only will archaeology as a profession suffer if we do not give the
public what it has paid for, but the chance to preserve the record of
the past may also be lost.

The above considerations may be briefly summed up. Contract archaeology seems to frequently operate on the premise that archaeology is easy.

In truth, contract archaeology, like all archaeology, is very difficult. Until we face this fact and deal with it accordingly, we cannot expect to do good archaeology or for the profession to advance.

There exists the question of whether it is client misunderstanding that forces contract archaeologists to occasionally operate in unsophisticated ways, or whether it stems from the archaeologists themselves. One could argue, however, that the question is moot. If the general public does not believe archaeology is difficult and requires high competence and innovation, etc. (and I think that many already do) they must be persuaded. So if there are discrepencies between what archaeologists feel should have been done and what they were actually in a position to do on a contract, this should be carefully explained in any subsequent reports so that the position of the archaeologist is made clear. Who is going to educate the public and administrators but us? We cannot blame them for our lack of teaching.

There are certainly sufficient situations in which archaeologists themselves have operated as if archaeology were quite simple, a situation which cannot be ascribed to the demands of their clients. For example, the number of EIR's, site surveys, and other clearances that are performed by minimally trained individuals is simply staggering. People totally new to entire regions are routinely sent out with little, if any, special training. Most of us know of examples of such practices spanning the breadth of the country. In the area where I am presently working well-trained crews who have spent a month or more surveying in a single valley still have difficulty picking out certain kinds of sites and features. It is not uncommon for M.A. level students to suddenly realize that they have walked over a 10,000 m^2 site without recognizing it, because it was of a type they had never previously encountered. How, then, can we believe that sending an unsupervised, improperly trained undergraduate on a clearance project is justifiable?

In fairness, of course, such unfortunate situations occur regardless of project funding, and it is not meant to be suggested that contract work is necessarily inferior to the average quality of archaeology being done today. It is, however, true that, in general, contract work is funded better than other kinds of archaeology at the same time the responsibilities are also greater. The removal of a small sample from a site which is not presently in danger of destruction, no matter how poorly done, does not do the same kind of harm as an "average" excavation of a major site, if the site is then totally destroyed and most of the artifacts discarded with a minimal amount of analysis. The very rationale underlying contract work requires higher standards than we might have for research-oriented excavations.

It would seem that this point is not being stressed with students of the discipline. There seems to be a psychological distaste for contract work in that it is perceived as being somehow less important or less real than pure academic archaeology. All efforts by government agencies and contract directors to increase professional standards will not convince professors that contract work is important for anthropology.

Conclusion

In conclusion, the ultimate responsibility for the quality and usefulness of contract archaeology rests with the academic side of archaeology. If this group of archaeologists can ignore the reality of contract work and feel they need not become involved, they are sadly in error. The problems of contract work are the problems of all of us. They must be considered in the archaeological curriculum not as special courses, but as parts of most courses. The role of students in contract work must be carefully considered by academia both for the sake of the students and the profession. The common relegation of contract work to the most junior faculty, graduate students, and professionals marginally associated with academia does not promote good archaeology or the eventual training of good archaeologists. It seems necessary to expect that all archaeologists devote some of their time to contract or salvage work either in the field as consultants, in the laboratory, or in the classroom. We must avoid the dichotomy between "establishment" academic archaeologists and "new rich" contract archaeologists.

Hopefully, it has been pointed out that many of the inherent problems in contract work can be solved by cooperation and innovative approaches. The problems do not primarily result from lack of funds, rather they are the result of a lack of concern by academic archaeologists. It would seem that those who have devoted the most to archaeology over the years ultimately have the most to lose if contract work becomes a stumbling block to doing quality archaeology and gaining a better understanding of the past.

REFERENCES

Clarke, David L.

    1972   A provisional model of an Iron Age society and its settlement system. In: David L. Clarke, ed., Models in Archaeology. London: Methuen, pp. 801-70.

Dittert, A.E., Jr., J. Hester, and F.W. Eddy

    1961   An archaeological survey of the Navajo reservoir district, monographs of the School of American Research and the Museum of New Mexico. No. 23. Santa Fe: School of American Research.

LeBlanc, Steven A.

    1975   Mimbres archaeological center: preliminary report of the first season of exavation, 1974. The Institute of Archaeology, University of California, Los Angeles.

LeBlanc, Steve A. and C. Khahil

    In press   Flare-Rimmed bowls: a sub type of Mimbres classic black on white. The Kiva.

Lipe, William D.

    1974   A conservation model for American archaeology. The Kiva 39(3-4):213-45.